THE
WORLD HISTORY
WORKBOOK

THE ANCIENT WORLD TO THE PRESENT

THE WORLD HISTORY WORKBOOK

Second Edition

David Hertzel

ROWMAN & LITTLEFIELD
Lanham • Boulder • New York • London

Published by Rowman & Littlefield
A wholly owned subsidary of The Rowman & Littlefield Publishing Group, Inc.
4501 Forbes Boulevard, Suite 200, Lanham, Maryland 20706
www.rowman.com

Unit A, Whitacre Mews, 26-34 Stannary Street, London SE11 4AB, United Kingdom

British Library Cataloguing in Publication Information Available

Library of Congress Cataloging-in-Publication Data
Names: Hertzel, David, author.
Title: The world history workbook : the ancient world to the present / David Hertzel.
Description: Second edition. | Lanham, MD : Rowman & Littlefield, [2016]
Identifiers: LCCN 2016004885 (print) | LCCN 2016004988 (ebook) | ISBN
    9781442251946 (pbk. : alk. paper) | ISBN 9781442251953 (electronic)
Subjects: LCSH: World history—Textbooks.
Classification: LCC D21 .H56 2016 (print) | LCC D21 (ebook) | DDC 909—dc23
LC record available at http://lccn.loc.gov/2016004885

Printed in the United States of America

But then, if I am right, certain professors of education must be wrong when they say that they can put a knowledge into the soul which was not there before, like sight into blind eyes.

—From the dialogue of Plato's *Republic*

Contents

Projects

Introduction

THIS SECOND edition of *The World History Workbook* introduces several new projects, project questions, and primary sources, combined into a single volume. The updated edition also organizes the modern narrative chronologically to facilitate its use as a companion alongside a more standard world history textbook. The workbook will still serve nicely as a stand-alone text, and many instructors will continue to use it in this way. But the new organization will allow the book's unique features, such as the readings on personal accountability and the student-centered approach to many of the projects, to be integrated into a more traditional narrative.

That humanity has a shared history is the guiding argument of *The World History Workbook*. World history reflects the heritage and history of every student's own family, culture, language, and values, and classroom discussions and textbook readings can demonstrate that students and faculty alike share with all people universal attributes, stories, and experiences. One of the goals of the workbook remains to encourage every student to be both humbled and dignified by the close connection he and she hold to the rest of humanity, for better and for worse. These goals have now been tested in university classrooms around the country for many years. The second edition emphasizes the methods and ideas which have received the most encouragement from world history faculty.

In the first two chapters especially, the readings and projects encourage students to examine aspects of the human experience that are universal, including language and the unified heritage of languages; genealogy; myth and myth types; literature and particular motifs and themes of literature; archetypes; and features of religion. As each of these topics is vast and worthy of extensive attention, rather than attempt an exhaustive coverage, the workbook provides historical examples as models around which instructors and students might build discussions suitable to the time and circumstances of their particular classes.

The subsequent chapters of *The World History Workbook* examine choices people make to distinguish themselves from or to cooperate with contrasting societies and people. The book asks students to consider contrasting interpretations of freedom, the individual, the self, and civilization and to discuss how various interpretations of civilization are reflected in tangible, historical examples. The final chapters show how in the modern age, the disparate histories of all people are merging into a shared, global experience with many benefits and many dangers. Processes of connections and exchange have been active throughout history, but the industrializing world has increased the pace of globalization such that in the course of the nineteenth, twentieth, and twenty-first centuries, time and space between societies have been reduced to a degree not seen for thousands of years—not since our ancestors lived in a geographically small area on the coast of Africa. World history and this textbook trace some paths along this story, from the people of the ancient world of Blombos Caves to the classrooms of modern universities, in the hope of contributing to a better future for us all.

CHAPTER 1

What Is History?

HISTORY MEANS two things: the events of the past and the study of the events of the past. Neither aspect of history can be understood without an appreciation for the other. When studying the past, one must have knowledge of events, but one must also understand something about the way to study, the way historians work. This text will give you an opportunity to evaluate past events and to use some of the methods historians use when analyzing history.

Historians look at the past by studying sources. There are two types of sources, primary and secondary. While these terms have somewhat different meanings in different disciplines, to historians, primary sources are things produced by the culture under examination. **Secondary sources** are published interpretations of primary sources. You will encounter both types of sources in this world history course, with most of the primary sources printed in the appendix at the end of this book. The text you are now reading is a secondary source.

Primary sources can include anything produced, built, written, painted, carved, narrated, or even left behind as refuse. In the modern world, written sources are very common and of probably the greatest use for historians. Written sources are rich and varied and can include books, poems, prayers, inscriptions, census or other reports, speeches, diaries, and newspapers. People produce other types of sources also useful to historians: art, graves, clothing, oral traditions, architecture, tools, and other technologies. To a historian, any and all of these products are potential primary sources that help us understand and interpret societies from the past.

Think of your own world. If you were to list artifacts that describe or define your own society, you might include an issue of a local newspaper, an office building, a census report, a car, a high school yearbook, a television show, some CDs, or a prayer book. Collectively, such a set would constitute a nice collection of sources that, when interpreted in context, could provide a reasonable description of your world. A local newspaper could show the types of news people in your world found important. It could show what movies were showing, the value of real estate, what types of crimes and punishments were committed. An office building could show how people worked, what types of building materials were used, and other things about architecture and public or private spaces. A census report might show population numbers, the average age of marriage, the attention your society paid to ethnic background. By piecing together information from all these sources, a scholar might reconstruct a picture of modern American society. But many questions would be left unanswered.

No source provides the complete truth about the past. In fact, historians rarely discuss "the truth" or "facts" at all, preferring instead to talk of "a truth" or "interpretations" of history. Any article, report, artifact, or technology can potentially be understood in many ways. A newspaper article contains bias; it might exclude information; it might have an angle that, if not interpreted in proper context, misleads the reader. For this reason, historians study as many sources as possible on a given subject. It is bad historical practice to ignore or discount a source simply because it is selective or misleading. A biased account is an excellent source on bias.

During the First World War, a war fought in Europe from 1914 until 1918 with Germany and Austria on one side and Great Britain, France, and the United States on the other (and Italy and Russia coming and going in between), daily and weekly newspapers reported on the war's progress. A regular feature of such reports described incredible atrocities committed by soldiers from enemy countries. French, British, and American papers ran articles describing atrocities of German and Austrian soldiers, while German papers ran articles describing atrocities of the Americans, the French, and the British. "News" articles described soldiers hacking nuns to death with pitchforks or throwing babies into the air and then catching them on the tips of swords, and other horrific things. One suspicious feature of these stories was how similar they were from country to country, regardless of the nationality of soldiers involved. A second suspicious feature was that such stories invariably concluded with declarations that the troops from the other side were "barbarians" who wished to crush the "civilized world." Such accounts avoided corroborating evidence and rarely mentioned independent sources. The fact is, the great majority of these accounts were simply false or were based on wildly exaggerated rumors. In all countries, newspapers ran the stories as **propaganda** to demonize an enemy and thus justify a war that was itself an atrocity and became increasingly awkward for leaders to explain. But historians do not dismiss outrageous newspaper sources simply because articles do not provide accurate accounts. On the contrary, such stories will always tell a truth of some kind, even when they are not accurate. These particular sources demonstrate mentalities of the time, the language of "barbarian" and "civilized" used on all sides, and the popular stereotypes of national groups. Historians know that every source has a story to tell but must be considered in light of a range of sources and evidence.

PROJECT 1
Primary Sources and Interpretations

Directions: List two primary sources to leave for future historians. The project has two parts: first, to identify specific sources you think are in some way representative of your own culture and society. These would be primary sources to the historian who would eventually examine them. Second, provide interpretations of the sources you list to advise scholars of the future how best to understand their meanings. In the spaces provided, list two specific primary sources by name, dates the sources were produced, and, where appropriate, page numbers. For example, "the Student Union building on the campus of [a specific university in a specific city] in use during 2015–2016"; and the movie *Iron Man 3*, released in 2013. The items you list should be real, traceable documents or artifacts. After each of the two items, write a short interpretation of that source. What information does that source show about the society that produced it? The more interpretive your answer, the better. For example, it would be a stronger statement to write that "the Student Union building" shows the value American society places on higher education than to say we know how to make buildings. It is a stronger argument to interpret the use of a building in terms of its social importance, the resources allocated, the way people looked at the building in contrast to other buildings, and so forth. It would be a stronger argument to discuss the roles women play in *Iron Man 3* than to argue that people enjoy movies. The first source you identify should be a written source such as an article, a story, the lyrics to a song, or something similar.

PROJECT 1
Primary Sources and Interpretations

1. Written primary source (title):

   Citation (author, date of publication, publisher, page number if applicable):

   Interpretation:

2. Primary source:

   Date, location, use:

   Interpretation:

Probably the most common types of sources historians examine are written. Written texts provide evidence for historical arguments in much the same way written documents provide evidence for cases in a court of law. It is not always obvious what interpretations a text might support. For example, look at the **Code of Hammurabi** (appendix 20), one of the world's oldest surviving written texts. The code outlines laws for ancient Mesopotamia and is naturally interpreted as a legal text. But the code provides insight beyond the legal sphere, into many aspects of life, family, and society in the ancient world.

Historians interpret texts by examining them critically, which is the same as saying historians use **critical thinking**. This means historians try to interpret sources without prejudice or judging. A historical source can be understood only if the bias of the present is set aside and the historian works objectively. Conventionally, this means to consider a text in context and comparison. *Context* means to place the text in its own environment, circumstances, standards, and values. To *compare* means to consider a source in contrast to other sources or texts, to other people, or to other circumstances, similar or dissimilar.

Historians try to set aside personal biases toward sources. *Like, dislike, boring, good, bad,* and similar terms of preference are not useful categories of analysis and can interfere with reasonable interpretations of *significance, consequences, causes,* and so on. Of course, historians prefer to work with texts they enjoy or find interesting or beautiful, but personal feelings should not influence interpretations of texts any more than a botanist's love of butterflies should influence a study of a butterfly's nervous system.

The Code of Hammurabi is significant in part because it was one of the earliest written (**codified**) laws. A written law is more accountable than an oral law or the personal ruler who governs on whim or inspiration. A written law can be discussed objectively; it has a record and a wording that is constant. This is not to say that written laws are applied uniformly or consistently; they are not. But a codified law has the opportunity for greater accountability. The Code of Hammurabi was engraved in stone and placed in public for all citizens to see.

PROJECT 2
Interpreting Historical Sources

A. Read the Code of Hammurabi in appendix 20. Answer each of the following questions, and then identify the verse that best supports your answer. You need not identify every reference, but the verses you cite must apply directly to the terms of the question you are answering.

(Example: "Mesopotamian society had both kings and slaves."

Answer: "Yes, Mesopotamian society had both kings and slaves. Passage 16 of the Code of Hammurabi mentions slaves while passage 129 refers to both kings and slaves.")

1. Women and men were treated equally under the law of Hammurabi.

2. In ancient Mesopotamia a woman could own a business.

3. People of different classes were treated equally under the law of Hammurabi.

B. Can modern historians have the moral authority to judge whether or not a law was "harsh," "unfair," or "unreasoned"?

To most modern observers, the Code of Hammurabi appears to be harsh and less than fair. But the law was also a product of its time. Consider the following two laws from another code from the ancient world, the Torah, the law of Moses and the people of Israel. These two selected laws are not necessarily representative of the larger body of Jewish law; instead, they have been chosen as examples of the severity of ancient laws.

From Deuteronomy 21:

18: If a man have a stubborn and rebellious son, which will not obey the voice of his father, or the voice of his mother, and that, when they have chastened him, will not hearken unto them:

19: Then shall his father and his mother lay hold on him, and bring him out unto the elders of his city, and unto the gate of his place;

20: And they shall say unto the elders of his city, This our son is stubborn and rebellious, he will not obey our voice; he is a glutton, and a drunkard.

21: And all the men of his city shall stone him with stones, that he die: so shalt thou put evil away from among you; and all Israel shall hear, and fear.

From Deuteronomy 22:

28: If a man find a damsel that is a virgin, which is not betrothed, and lay hold on her, and lie with her, and they be found;

29: Then the man that lay with her shall give unto the damsel's father fifty shekels of silver, and she shall be his wife; because he hath humbled her, he may not put her away all his days.

1. Is it possible to *argue* that some of the laws from Hammurabi and Moses are unfair or unjust? Or, does a historian need to stay always aloof and accept that "other people had other customs," which might have been "fair" to them but not to us?

2. How might modern Jewish theologians or believers reconcile their belief in the Torah as a sacred text and at the same time defend a modern human rights agenda?

In project 2, you provided evidence to support historical arguments. Your arguments are interpretations of the Code of Hammurabi, the Torah, fairness, and so on.

An **argument** is an opinion one is prepared to defend using evidence. Without evidence, an argument becomes bare opinion, or **assertion**. Historians use many types of evidence in forming and defending arguments, and no evidence should be dismissed without some consideration. Any time evidence is deliberately ignored, hidden, or refused without due consideration, historical accuracy suffers. Historians need to be accountable to their sources. This means that historians must honestly consider all the available evidence in the same way a court of law needs to consider all evidence relevant to a particular case. The misuse of evidence makes bad historical research in much the same way misuse of evidence can lead to wrong decisions in a court of law.

An example of overtly bad history is the work of so-called **Holocaust deniers**. While revisionist historians (**revisionism**) are those who revise interpretations of history on the basis of new evidence or new interpretations of old evidence, Holocaust deniers simply refuse to consider evidence for the historical mass extermination of Jews in Europe under Nazi rule. Since the whole body of evidence overwhelmingly opposes their position, deniers dismiss large bodies of sources they claim must be biased. Jewish sources, or sources that come from Jewish victims, Holocaust deniers claim, are unreliable and cannot be considered because they come from Jewish sources. But as we have already shown, even in cases where sources show bias or inaccuracies, responsible historians do not exclude evidence by group. This would be similar to dismissing all Native American sources from the history of the United States on the premise that Native sources must be overwhelmingly distorted in favor of Native perspectives. Yet there is no evidence to show that either Native Americans or Jews are any less capable of, or are less likely to provide, objective testimony than are people from other groups. In any case, even when historians encounter bias in a particular text, they do not dismiss the source; they use it for what truth it offers. Most sources have something to contribute to a reconstruction of the past, though not perhaps always in keeping with the intentions of the witness. Responsible historians interpret texts; they do not dispose of them.

When white Europeans began to explore the African interior in the eighteenth century, they discovered ruins and remains they did not expect to find. Europeans of the time were educated to believe not only that European societies were superior to all other societies but also that there was no civilization in most of the world until Europeans arrived. European scholars and explorers refused to believe that any culture that did not look like European culture could possibly be defined as "civilized." Therefore, when Europeans went in search of new worlds, they looked for features familiar to them as evidence for "civilization." For Europeans, these features included permanent buildings, institutions, and scientific mentalities. When they found people living in huts or yurts, in migrant circumstances, and without technologies as fast and as powerful as those of European industry, Europeans claimed the cultures they encountered did not "yet" have civilization. They also presumed that since all people "naturally" prefer civilization, native people must be incapable of producing such things or they would have already produced them. Eventually this thinking became part of a racial interpretation of the world. In other words, the cultural arrogance of European societies merged with contemporary racial theories to produce a general perception that the determining feature of civilization was "race" (defined by skin color).

So when European explorers arrived at a place in Africa called **Zimbabwe**, they were baffled. There they found the ruins of a great city built of stone, with permanence and a technology capable of heavy construction. Ideally scholars would have examined the ruins with objectivity, treating artifacts and remains carefully, examining them critically. But because of their racial preconceptions, Europeans almost universally declared it impossible that the cities of Zimbabwe could have been built by native people of the region. Zimbabwe, Europeans argued, must have been built by non-African people, perhaps Europeans, perhaps some biblical people. General agreement settled on the theory that the Queen of Sheba had built Great Zimbabwe. There was no solid evidence for this theory, but intellectual prejudice obscured the evidence. For more than a century this theory held fast, during which time most of the local archeological sites were devastated by adventurers and gold seekers. People destroyed or looted evidence to such an extent that by the end of the nineteenth century, very little remained visible of ancient Zimbabwe but architectural remains. Eventually two twentieth-century archeologists were able, through investigations of neighboring, less disturbed sites, to determine that Zimbabwe was built by **Shona** people, native to the region, whose descendants still live in the area today. But for many years historians, archeologists, and anthropologists taught and believed completely false histories of the central regions of Africa. If researchers and scholars had paid closer and more honest attention to the evidence and had remained true to their sources, there would have been no need for this error.

In general, it is possible to classify historical interpretations and evidence by quality into two categories, **historical** and **unhistorical**. For the most part, historical refers to objective evidence while unhistorical refers to subjective evidence. *Historical* in this sense describes something verifiable, something observable or testable, using reason. *Unhistorical*, on the other hand, does not mean necessarily untrue; rather, it signifies a position adopted and accepted on faith (trust) but that cannot be tested or verified. Unhistorical things are accepted on belief, not on evidence. So while historians might not commonly speak about the "facts of history," they do refer to an argument or a source as historical or unhistorical.

Consider an account of a personal vision by the medieval Christian mystic **Hildegard of Bingen**, a nun from southern Germany. Hildegard recorded numerous visions she believed to have come from God or from a "messenger of God." She wrote in the twelfth century in a letter to her friend Abbot Phillip,

> A wind blew from a high mountain and, as it passed over ornamented castles and towers, it put into motion a small feather which had no ability of its own to fly but received its movement entirely from the wind. Surely the almighty God arranged this to show what the Divine could achieve through a creature that had no hope of achieving anything by itself.[1]

The source includes historical information, such as the fact that Hildegard wrote the letter to her friend, she described visions, she personally associated those visions with God, and she was aware of castles and towers. Her descriptions of visions might be interpreted psychologically, medically, or spiritually. Historians interpret in all these ways; responsible historians interpret in context and by using all objective evidence available. It would be unhistorical, however, to argue that Hildegard actually received her visions from God or that she in fact flew around the countryside in the form of a feather. Her visions may or may not have come from God, but in either case, it would be unhistorical to say so. It is not within the scope of historical analysis to maintain that Hildegard's vision came from God one way or the other, as this would be a subjective judgment, a statement of belief. Historians should avoid making subjective and personal judgments. Neither should scholars of any discipline mock or deny historical figures and culture the beliefs they held. An argument is not a moral judgment. Hildegard's descriptions are important and valuable as historical sources; it is not within the scope of the historian's work to argue whether they were real or false.

It sometimes might appear that a person who "was there" to experience firsthand a historical event has more authority than "circumstantial" evidence. For historians, however, this is rarely the case; objective evidence is typically more reliable than isolated firsthand accounts. Firsthand testimonies are notoriously unreliable and must match the objective evidence before being accepted. Think of a person's own account of a car accident. Should the courts accept all eyewitness testimony simply because a person "was there"? Since people commonly provide false testimony for many

---

1. Hildegard of Bingen and Matthew Fox, *Book of Divine Works* (Santa Fe: Bear, 1987), 320.

reasons, including bad memories, courts, like historians, will override personal testimonies that contradict disinterested evidence. Just because a friend insists he was abducted by aliens does not make it true. Most of us would require physical evidence to support a personal account. So it is with history. First-person evidence is not always historically reliable.

PROJECT 3
Historical and Unhistorical, Arguments and Assertions

A. Next to each short event or account, write either *historical* or *unhistorical*. There is a correct answer to each one.

1. George Washington never told a lie.

2. Hildegard of Bingen had visions from God.

3. Hildegard of Bingen wrote about visions from God.

4. Native African people are not capable of constructing with stone.

5. Romans built roads.

6. Romans loved the true God.

7. Romans built temples to their gods.

8. John Kennedy was the best president.

9. Bill Clinton ran as the presidential candidate of the Democratic Party.

(continued)

B. What is the qualitative difference between the contrasting sets of terms in the two columns?

argument	assertion
objective	subjective
historical	unhistorical
reason	faith
evidence	belief

Secondary sources are arguments (interpretations) of history, usually based on primary sources. While all historians should be accountable to sources, some historians also find patterns of causality in history. **Causality** means the relationship between cause and effect, or what caused an event, a transition, or a development to occur. For example, what caused people to settle into farming communities in one area but not in another? Why did one society explore the oceans and the other society not? How did religions develop, and why, in the patterns they did? When historians study such questions, they sometimes look for patterns to causes, and not only to causes, for individual events. Patterns of causality regular enough to be predictable are known as **determinism**. Determinism suggests an inevitability of events; that is, things had to happen the way they did. In other words, given the determining factors in place at a particular time, the outcome that did occur must have occurred. For example, given the historical conditions (determinants) in place prior to the First World War (nationalism, industrialism, capitalism, and so on), the First World War was unavoidable. Not all historians use determinism; some find determinism restricting, but all historians examine cause and effect.

Probably the most familiar form of determinism is known as **economic determinism**. Economic determinism is an interpretation that looks for economic conditions to trigger behavior or change in history. The argument that a presidential election will be determined by the state of relations between economic groups is an argument an economic determinist might make. There are some well-known examples of arguments based on economic determinism. Two examples are that society is usually formed into economic classes and that revolutions are motivated by economic circumstances. These two arguments come from **Karl Marx**, the founder of economic determinism. Marx described the whole scope of history in economic terms, with ruling classes controlling wealth and property and working classes producing wealth for the ruling classes. Marx wrote his famous works on **capital and labor** (ruling classes and producing classes, respectively) during the industrial revolutions of the mid- and late eighteen hundreds, a time when tensions between workers and industry was great and capitalist greed and abuse seemed unchecked. Some of Marx's specific views have become outdated in the twenty-first century, but Marx's economic constructions survive as influential interpretations of society and history.

A second determinism has survived almost exclusively in the sphere of popular history; that is, in places such as history on television, or so-called *historical fiction*. This second determinism is called **Great Men and Battles**. Like Karl Marx's economic determinism, this method was developed during the nineteenth century, but in this case by nationalist writers from Europe to create grand myths about the heritage of a country. No serious scholar today uses this outdated determinism. One reason it continues to capture the imagination of the popular audience is its compelling use of glory and drama. Consider the inspiring opening passage from an essay by the nineteenth-century historian **Sir Edward Creasy**. Creasy included his account of the **Battle of Marathon** in his famous 1857 work titled *Fifteen Decisive Battles of the World*. Marathon was one of the most complete victories of the ancient Greeks over the Persians.

> Two thousand three hundred and forty years ago a council of Athenian officers was summoned on the slope of one of the mountains that look over the plain of Marathon, on the eastern coast of Attica. The immediate subject of their meeting was to consider whether they should give battle to an enemy that lay encamped on the shore beneath them; but on the result of their deliberations depended, not merely the fate of two armies, but the whole future progress of human civilization.

Creasy further explains,

> The day of Marathon . . . broke forever the spell of Persian invincibility, which had paralyzed men's minds. . . . It secured for mankind the intellectual treasures of Athens, the growth of free institutions, the liberal enlightenment of the western world and the gradual ascendancy for many ages of the great principles of European civilization.[2]

Creasy was a wonderful writer, but his historical interpretations are no longer taken seriously. Historians today look at many more factors to describe the rise and fall of empires or the establishment of democratic institutions in England. Creasy's argument suggests that the victory of the Greeks over the Persians at Marathon caused the survival of democratic traditions in ancient Athens, which in turn led to a European "Western tradition," which in turn led to the rise of Great Britain as a world power fifteen centuries later. If Creasy's analysis is correct, however, every contingency that led to the Battle of Marathon must also have led to the rise of democratic institutions in Great Britain. Every other detail that provided for an Athenian victory must also have led to English greatness: the use of hoplites, the institution of slavery in Greece, the diet and culture of the Greeks that produced such excellent soldiers, including the prevalent homosexual lifestyle of the ancient soldiers. Obviously, such obscure connections are tenuous, and the argument breaks down when it is examined more closely. But Creasy's point was really to glorify his nation's own history by associating it with a romantic past.

Perhaps more recent historical methods are somewhat more boring than Great Men and Battles, but recent methods are more honest, inclusive,

---

2. Sir Edward Creasy, *Fifteen Decisive Battles of the World* (Harrisburg, PA: Military Service Publications, 1943), 1.

and accurate. Until the middle of the twentieth century, modern historical research was dominated by national or topical history. In the past fifty years or so, however, historians have begun to broaden the narrative to include groups, people, and institutions that had been previously marginalized. Historians of the 1950s and 1960s began to recognize the importance to history of everyday life and people, including those who do not command positions of power and public authority. Historians began to write history to reflect the social reality that all elements of society contribute to the makeup and development of human civilization. It has now become conventional to integrate into the historical analysis families, minor institutions, popular mentalities, and statistics as well as people of power. This way of describing the past is more democratic and more realistic than previous, elitist methods. The new inclusive histories are called *social history*.

Thus we see that history changes with society; as the world democratized, so did history become more **inclusive** (democratic). As the world globalized, so did the study of history. Many historians felt that to be intellectually honest and to keep pace with current developments in historical research, university curricula must integrate into general education programs at universities in the United States more of the world than had been previously considered. During the 1990s, many history departments changed Western civilization or "great texts" course requirements to world history requirements. This trend followed a twentieth-century pattern of globalization, accelerated by innovations in computers, space exploration, and the Internet. This text and this approach to world history are reflections of the changing world. By participating in this course, you are involved in both the changing world and the changing ways history is evaluated and written.

PROJECT 4
Methods Historians Use

Use complete sentences to answer the questions below.

1. What inherent weaknesses might come with determinisms?

2. What are some possible strengths of the use of determinisms in interpreting history?

GENRE

Historians study within particular **genres**, or areas. Areas of study are sometimes national, such as American history or Russian history. National studies can help define a nation or people, correct misconceptions, or generate discussion about national experience. But historians are not mythmakers; they are interpreters of the past and formulate arguments on the basis of sound reasoning. It is not the work of scholars to praise a national history simply out of a sense of nationalism. Historians do not best engage in preaching, whitewashing, or sugarcoating. If a state or people have positive and negative aspects in their past, historians should be free to address both rationally and in proper context. Japanese historians have recently come under strong criticism, for example, for ignoring in school textbooks the violent behavior of the Japanese occupation of China in the middle of the past century. The Chinese government wants Japanese students to be taught honestly about the Japanese past, perhaps in order to prevent future atrocities. It is partly the work of historians to be sure accurate accounts are available.

Larger geographic regions than "country" might also define historical categories. Geography in all its aspects—climate, wildlife, landscape, and natural resources—influences the way people eat, travel, and communicate; the materials they use; the art they make; and the size of families they raise. Some historians therefore study history within this important framework. One such focus of study and teaching is the **Atlantic World**. This large area supersedes national boundaries and includes the eastern regions of the Americas and the western regions of Africa and Europe. The Atlantic World saw enormous population shifts during the centuries following 1492. Through the massive importation of slaves from Africa, settlers' arrival from Europe, and the violent reduction of native populations, the ethnic and cultural makeup of both the northern and southern Americas changed forever. Patterns of change in North America differed in some respects from those in Central and South America, but overall patterns of slavery, settlement, and nation building spanned the western side of the Atlantic. The history of every nation of Latin America rests on the experiences of those first centuries of contact. Arguments historians might make regarding the Atlantic World address the degree and type of African influence on the culture of Brazil, for example, or might ask to what degree South American native cultures influenced West Africa. Certainly massive economic changes resulted from the slave trade, not to mention the violent loss of populations to Atlantic slavery. The Atlantic World is only one of several such supranational geographic regions historians recognize as fields of study. Others include the Mediterranean and the Silk Road.

Other genres of history help define interaction among historical groups. Women's history examines how societies have defined women and family, citizenship, and culture in the context of gender. **Big history** studies the whole of human history in the context of the universe, the natural world, the ecology of the planet, and the impact humans have had on the environment. There are also specialized fields of history such as economic history or the history of slavery, technology, science, and so on. In short, historians can research and teach almost any aspect of the human experience.

Critical Thinking, Justice, Faith, and Reason

1. Is justice dependent on critical thinking?

CHAPTER 2

The Grand Narrative
Universals in History

ARCHEOLOGISTS GENERALLY agree that a couple million years ago an **anatomically modern human** emerged from previous primates and roamed the planet hunting, gathering, and fishing. This creature was physically identical to people of today but does not appear to have been behaviorally exactly like us. Early anatomically modern humans did not build permanent settlements and neither farmed nor domesticated animals. Their religious practice is uncertain, and in archeological remains there is little direct evidence of a creative person; these early humans did not create art, neither did they establish deliberate political organization or religious traditions.

Sometime around three hundred thousand to one hundred thousand years ago, however, emerged the **behaviorally modern human**; not a new species, but the same creature as its anatomical predecessor except in behavior. What caused a change in the primate is not known, but there is widespread scholarly agreement that what was new was the appearance of abstract thought. Most archeologists and anthropologists maintain that the first behaviorally modern people lived in eastern Africa and were the direct ancestors to all people alive today. When behaviorally modern people appeared can probably not be reduced to a single year or even a single century but should probably be thought of as a gradual development. New discoveries have pushed the dating of our abstract-thinking ancestors further and further back. Currently the oldest archeological site showing strong evidence of abstract thought has been dated at around seventy thousand years ago. This site, at **Blombos Cave** in southern Africa, contains tools for fishing and other items that could be found at earlier sites. But the people of the coastal caves left behind something else: a small stone, engraved with an abstract pattern.

The markings on this small piece of ochre might look crude, but they are clearly deliberate. Someone made these etchings to represent something,

Blombos Cave Art. Courtesy of the National Science Foundation.

to communicate something. To us the precise meaning is lost, but the artist's handiwork carries to us a new meaning from seventy thousand years past: the people of Blombos Cave thought abstractly and expressed themselves abstractly. The two articles in appendix 19 that deal with the discoveries at Blombos Cave report that to most modern scientists, what distinguishes humans from animals and behaviorally modern humans from their ancestors is abstract thought. But naming **abstract thinking** as the defining and unique feature of human beings is not universally accepted. Some argue that modern humans have free will, and that is what distinguishes them from other creatures. Others maintain that toolmaking or use of complex language defines modern humans. One of the problems in distinguishing humans from animals is that there is evidence that some animals also have abilities to think abstractly, to make tools, or to use complex language, for example.

The reason Karl Marx wrote history as an economic narrative is that Marx understood humans as economic creatures. For Sigmund Freud, on the other hand, the history of humanity is a psychological struggle, because Freud understood humans as psychological creatures. For the nineteenth-century Europeans in Africa, described in the previous chapter, humans were racial creatures (among other things), making history a racial and national narrative. Whatever the nature of humanity, history will be written accordingly. Human nature guides human history, and how one understands human nature informs how one understands history. But defining a human nature is difficult.

The people of Blombos Cave in Africa were early creators of culture, and this has been ever since one of the marks of all human societies. Culture includes all those things Marx, Freud, and the archeologists identified and more. First, humans create **material culture**, which provides food, shelter, and clothing. Beyond that, culture extends to social, political, and religious needs. Every human group since Blombos Cave (and perhaps earlier) has devised ways to provide for material, social, and religious needs. No human society can be said to have "more" culture than any other, though each fashions culture uniquely. One society uses a bagpipe, the other a lute, the other a drum. But all create music. One paints while another sculpts, but all have art. In this way, the work of being human is different throughout time and around the world, but it is also very similar from people to people.

Where features are common to every society, we call this a **universal**. While societies frequently boast about and even go to war over differences, many aspects of culture are actually universal. Language and literature, for example, represent cultural features that are distinct and at the same time universal. For while all people have language and literature, each culture creates its own version of language and literature, including oral traditions. By identifying commonalities we can see that culture is as potentially unifying as it is dividing.

PROJECT 6
Human, What Makes You Human?

Is there some quality or behavior which sets human beings apart from other creatures? Look to yourself. In complete sentences and from your own experience, identify something you do or have done that identifies you as a human being, something you believe no other creature does naturally. Explain what that behavior or action represents, which defines a human. Is that part of a human nature?

THE PARADOX OF GENEALOGY

An examination of genealogy shows that humans are universally related by family. Genealogists trace a family's ancestry, usually following direct (genetic) lines (parents to grandparents, to great-grandparents, etc.). This method shows the uniqueness of each family line. But a slightly broader perspective reveals that no person—let alone people—possesses a discrete ancestry, segregated from those of other families. Every family on earth is in fact related to every other family. Using the chart that follows, consider the mathematical implications of the proposition that each person possesses an isolated genealogy. The chart is based on a simple formula: one generation averages twenty-five years, and every person has two parents, who in turn have two parents each, and so on. Fill in the numbers in each column.

Column 1, *Generations Back*, numbers the generations beginning with 1, a set of parents, then 2, the grandparents, and so on. The second column dates that generation using a formula of one generation equals twenty-five years. This is an approximation but will average out over time. The third column, named *Number of Direct Line Ancestors*, counts the number of direct line ancestors who would have lived in each of those generations following the count of one person, two parents. Therefore, there are two (parents) in the first generation, four (grandparents) in the second generation back, and so on.

PROJECT 7
The Paradox of Genealogy

Fill in the blank lines with correct figures.

Generations Back	Years Ago (# of generations × 25 yrs) / Date	# of Direct Line Ancestors
1	25 / 1975	2 (parents)
2	50 / 1950	4
3		
4		
5		
6		
7		
8		
9		
10		
11		
12		
13		
14		
15		
16		
17		
18		
19		
20		
21		
22		
23		

(*continued*)

Generations Back	Years Ago (# of generations × 25 yrs) / Date	# of Direct Line Ancestors
24		
25		
26		
27		
28		
29		
30		
31		
32		

It should be plain to see the chart cannot be correct. Not only does the number in column 3 increase to impossible proportions, but according to this formula, the farther we go into the past on the chart, the larger the population. Yet we know that at some point in the past, the population of the world was much smaller than it is today, perhaps no larger than a few people.

The solution to this **paradox of genealogy** is that we are all descended from the same people and that we are descended many times over (that is, through multiple lines) from the same ancestors. Families intermarry, cousins marry cousins, second cousins marry and have children, and so on. Children of a pair of first cousins, for example, have six great-grandparents each rather than the eight the chart would indicate. The same would be true of second cousins, regarding great-great-grandparents. So while it is correct to say that all people are descended 1,024 times ten generations back, it does not follow that individuals have 1,024 direct-line, distinct ancestors in the tenth generation.

Extrapolate this solution to larger numbers of people, and a remarkable picture emerges: all people are genealogically cousins. One need not go very far into the past to identify ancestors common to large groups of people, even nations, continents, and eventually the entire population of the world. Mathematicians working on these problems conclude that every person alive with even a single European, North African, or Middle Eastern ancestor, for example, is directly descended from Muhammad, the prophet of Islam, and from Charlemagne, the king of the Franks. Muhammad lived in the eighth century, Charlemagne in the ninth. Go back a few centuries and you will find people who are ancestors to every person on earth. We are likely all the descendants of Queen Nefertiti of ancient Egypt, for example, and Confucius is our genealogical grandparent as well.

PROJECT 8
In Your Own Words, Summarize the Paradox of Genealogy

1. Describe the paradox of genealogy.

2. Explain the solution to the paradox.

3. Explain the implications of the solution to the paradox to the modern concept of race.

Discovering the links and naming the ancestors is exciting and honorable work. But even those without a documented genealogy can rest assured they share ancestry with every group of people on earth. We are cousins not only in "spirit" or culture but in DNA and family.

LANGUAGE

The three concepts of language, culture, and people are so intimately related they are used synonymously. *German* can indicate German people, German language, or German culture. The same is true of *Japanese*, *Thai*, and many others as well; one word names all three things.

Traditions of language and culture are conventionally discussed in national terms, such as *German literature*, *Japanese literature*, and so on. National lines define literature not exactly by nation, however, but more often by language, which transcends state boundaries. In German literary traditions, for example, one will find Franz Kafka, who wrote in German but was from the Czech city of Prague. German Jews such as Heinrich Heine, who wrote in German, are also conventionally included in the German literary tradition, whereas German émigrés who wrote in English or in the language of an adopted country might be found in traditions of both Germany and the United States. Thus, not all writers of German are Germans, and not all those who are Germans write in the German language. The same is true of "national literature" of the United States. American literature does not ordinarily include English-language literature of the British Isles or of Canada but might include Native American literature not in English. There is American literature in many languages: Spanish, Chinese, Tsalagi (Cherokee), and so on. In short, efforts to segregate culture "nationally" are contrived and open to flaw even in the most "national" of all characteristics, language.

To people from societies with writing, it might seem that given the opportunity, any society would naturally elect to have writing. But at least one civilization provides a different picture. The people who built ancient **Teotihuacan** of central Mesoamerica constructed cities and enormous temples, traded over great distances, and celebrated elaborate rituals. They performed these feats of engineering and organization with only very limited systems of writing. Yet the Teotihuacan traded regularly with people who used writing and presumably could have adopted writing for themselves. Historians have different theories about why the Teotihuacanos chose to not implement writing, but as yet, no one knows for certain.

Language is obviously universal. All people have language equally. Literature is also universal, in the absence of writing as much as with writing. And within literature there are also universals, recurrent themes that might appear in myths, rituals, stories, songs, prayers, and poems. One could find many particular themes in literature worldwide, some very specific, others more general. For example, the theme of "the pain of separation" appears in the literature of every human tradition. Pain and grief over separation from someone or something loved is expressed worldwide and throughout history in poems, songs, hymns, plays, rituals, and so forth. Separation from departed loved ones is perhaps the most common form this sentiment assumes, but humans can grieve separation from many things. For example, this medieval Hebrew poet wrote from Spain about the pain of being separated from his homeland. In so doing, he described a universal sentiment and theme.

Jerusalem
Beautiful heights, city of a great King,
From the western coast my desire burns towards thee.
Pity and tenderness burst in me, remembering
Thy former glories, thy temple now broken stones.
I wish I could fly to thee on the wings of an eagle
And mingle my tears with thy dust.
I have sought thee, love, though the King is not there
And instead of Gilead's balm, snakes and scorpions.
Let me fall on thy broken stones and tenderly kiss them—
The taste of thy dust will be sweeter than honey to me.

—Judah Halevi (trans. Robert Mezey)[1]

1. Robert Mezey, ed., *Poems from the Hebrew* (New York: Crowell, 1973), 62. Reprinted courtesy of Robert Mezey.

PROJECT 9
Universals in Literature I

Below are poems from five different cultural and literary traditions, distant from one another in space and time. Yet they share common themes, including the pain of separation.

Using an ink highlighter, mark phrases in each poem that show this universal theme, and indicate in the margin the separation the author describes.

To the Distant One

And have I lost thee evermore,
Hast thou, oh, fair one, from me flown?
Still in mine ear sounds, as of yore,
Thine every word, thine every tone.

As when at morn the wanderer's eye
Attempts to pierce the air in vain,
When, hidden in the azure sky,
The lark high o'er him chants his strain:

So do I cast my troubled gaze
Through bush, through forest, o'er the lea;
Thou art invoked by all my lays;
Oh, come then, loved one, back to me!

　　　　　—Johann Wolfgang von Goethe (German, 1749–1832)[2]

Mountain Spirit

The deer, when they fall to death,
Return to love of their wives.
The fields and hills, when they wither away,
Return to Spring a thousand years old.

　　　　　—Toson Shimazaki (Japan, 1880s)[3]

---

2. Johann Wolfgang von Goethe, *The Poems of Goethe, Translated in the Original Metres by Edgar Alfred Bowring*, trans. Edgar Alfred Bowring (London: J. W. Parker, 1853), 19.

3. Yone Noguchi, *The Spirit of Japanese Poetry* (London: John Murray, 1914), 94.

Li Fu-jen

The sound of her silk skirt has stopped.
On the marble pavement dust grows.
Her empty room is cold and still.
Fallen leaves are piled against the doors.
Longing for that lovely lady
How can I bring my aching heart to rest?

—Wu-ti (China, 157–87 BCE)[4]

(Untitled)

Violently falls the snow,
In the mist that precedes the lightning;
It bends the branches to the earth,
And splits the tallest trees in twain.
Among the shepherds none can pasture his flock;
It closes to traffic all the roads to market.
Lovers must then trust the birds,
With messages to their loves—
Messages to express their passion.

—Moorish (North Africa)[5]

Carrickfergus (stanzas 3 and 4)

My childhood days bring back sad reflections
of happy days so long ago.
My boyhood friends and my own relations,
have all passed on like the melting snow.
So I'll spend my days in endless roving,
soft is the grass and my bed is free.
Oh to be home now in Carrickfergus,
on the long road down to the salty sea.

—traditional (Ireland)[6]

---

4. Arthur Waley, *Translations from the Chinese* (New York: Knopf, 1919), 49.

5. Rene Basset, ed., *Moorish Literature* (New York: Collier, 1900), viii.

6. Lyrics traditional, from Van Morrison and the Chieftains, *Irish Heartbeat*, recorded 1987–88, Mercury 834 496-1.

Separation from one's homeland, loved ones, or family might seem like an obvious universal, but we could choose from many other examples of universals. Every literary tradition, whether oral or written, makes use of themes, symbols, and motifs. Particular themes and motifs occur over and over throughout the cultures of the world. There has been a great deal of research into comparative themes in myth, literature, and religions for more than a century. The great Swiss psychiatrist Carl Jung identified many universal motifs not only in literature but also in rituals, in dreams, and in religious traditions. For example, Jung identified the motif and symbol of wind or breeze as a universal signifier of life or soul. Jung called these universal motifs **archetypes** and maintained that human societies use archetypes as expressions of a unified human consciousness. "All the most powerful ideas of history go back to archetypes," wrote Jung. He included among archetypes the persona, the self, the old wise man, the trickster, and others.

MYTH

Myths are stories that are neither factual nor false but adhere instead to deeper truths. Myths can express social, political, or religious themes, or they can provide interpretations of the natural world. **Joseph Campbell**, a preeminent twentieth-century scholar of myth, claims mythmaking and human society emerged together. Evidence of myth found at the earliest archeological sites

> tells us something, furthermore, of the unity of our species; for the fundamental themes of mythological thought have remained constant and universal, not only throughout history, but also over the whole extent of mankind's occupation of the earth.[7]

Every society constructs myths. Some universal types include **hero myths**, **creation myths**, morality, quest, and myths that define social identity. Hero myths typically follow patterns of "(1) separation, (2) initiation, and (3) return." Campbell writes,

> A hero ventures forth from the world of common day into a region of supernatural wonder: fabulous forces are there encountered and a decisive victory is won: the hero comes back from this mysterious adventure with the power to bestow boons on his fellow men.[8]

In modern society, hero myths can be found in film, in religious stories, and in fiction. Even American "road trip" movies sometimes follow this ancient

7. Joseph Campbell, *Myths to Live By: The Emergence of Mankind* (Toronto: Bantam, 1972), 19.
8. Campbell, *Myths to Live By*, 209.

pattern, as do some parts of the *Lord of the Rings* and Harry Potter stories. Though people do not hold faith in these stories as they might a great traditional myth, the structures are similar, and the stories are instructive in that sense.

Creation myths describe origins. It seems to be an important element of any civilization to search for tribal or cultural origins and to explain human existence. Some of the world's richest collections of myths come from the people of the Americas, North and South. The following myth and prayer originates from one ancient civilization of the Andes. The prayer was translated into Spanish verse in the sixteenth century by Bishop Luis Geronimo de Ore. It was later translated into English.

> O Pachacamac!
> Thou who hast existed from the beginning.
> Thou who shalt exist until the end,
> powerful but merciful,
> Who didst create man by saying,
> "Let man be,"
> Who defended us from evil,
> and presented our life and our health,
> art Thou in the sky or upon the earth?
> In the clouds or in the deeps?
> Hear the voice of him who implores Thee,
> and grant him his petitions.
> Give us life everlasting,
> preserve us, and accept this our sacrifice.[9]

As they develop and evolve over long periods of time, myths often synthesize many elements and traditions into single accounts. This is the case of the **Popul Vuh**, the great myth of the Kiche **Maya** of Central America. This creation myth from the *Popul Vuh* shows at least four different traditions that had integrated into Kiche culture. It was translated from the Maya Kiche language by Lewis Spence.

> Over a universe wrapped in a gloom of a dense and primeval night passed the good Hurakan the mighty wind. He called out, "earth," and the solid land appeared. The chief gods took counsel; they were Hurakan, Gucumatz, the serpents covered with green feathers, and Xpiyacoc and Xmucane, the mother and father gods. As the result of their deliberations animals were created. But as yet man was not. To supply the deficiency the divine beings resolved to create mannikins

---

9. Millicent Todd Bingham, *Peru: A Land of Contrasts* (Boston: Little, Brown, 1914), 177–78.

carved out of wood. But these soon incurred the displeasure of the gods, who, irritated by their lack of reverence, resolved to destroy them. Then, by the will of Hurakan, the Heart of Heaven, the waters were swollen, and a great flood came across the mannikins of wood.[10]

The Christian influence in this creation myth is evident, but one can also see that the account draws from other traditions as well. Myths are reflections of the culture that produced them, deep, profound, intricate.

The intimate identification of a culture with its myths has led one scholar to refer to some myths as national sagas, such as the *Iliad* of the Greeks or the ***Mahabharata*** of India. The *Mahabharata* is several thousand years old and contains many types of myth within its narrative. The sacred text *Bhavagad Gita* is part of the *Mahabharata*, as are numerous national, moral, and hero myths. The *Mahabharata* opens with a simple story about a **Brahman**, or priest; turn to appendix 21 to read it.

---

10. Lewis Spence, *Mythic and Heroic Sagas of the Kiches of Central America* (London: D. Nutt, 1908), 9–10.

PROJECT 10
Myth and the *Mahabharata*

Although the selection is brief, the story from the *Mahabharata* provided in the appendix is suggestive and seems to be promising great things.

Describe in your own words, in sentences, how the opening of the *Mahabharata* contains all three elements of the hero myth.

PROJECT 11
Universals in Literature II

1. What theme or motif is common in the two selections below, and what does it signify?

   Answer: _____

   A Dance with the Breeze [partial]
   Sailing downward from the trees,
   Autumn leaves spin in a dance
   With the sportive autumn breeze,
   Whose soft music will enhance
   The enjoyment which they find,
   As they leave their summer home
   Traveling with the wayward wind,
   Over country fields, to roam.

   —Martha Shepard Lippincott (United States, 1928)[11]

   Men pass away since the time of Ra
   and the youths come in their stead.
   Like as Ra reappears every morning,
   and Tum sets in the horizon,
   men are begetting,
   and women are conceiving.
   Every nostril inhaleth once the breezes of dawn,
   but all born of women go down to their places.

   —from "The Song of the Harper" (Egypt)[12]

---

11. Martha Shepard Lippincott, "A Dance with the Breeze," *Education* 48, no. 6 (February 1928): 386.

12. "The Song of the Harper," in *Egyptian Literature*, ed. Epiphanius Wilson, trans. Ludwig Stern (New York: Colonial Press, 1901), 346.

THE GENEALOGY OF LANGUAGES

All languages can be traced back in time as one might trace a family along a genealogical tree, from generation to generation. And, as with people, if we could trace any language backward in time to its origins, we would arrive eventually in Africa, at a single ancestral language from which all people, all cultures, and all languages descend. The original mother language to all languages is called **First Language** and was probably spoken between one hundred thousand and two hundred thousand years ago.

Linguists reconstruct the relationships between languages by examining the parts of language such as words, syntax, and so on. Where linguists find sets of traits that are common to two languages, such as shared words, they can establish that the languages have come into contact with each other or share a common ancestry. For example, the English and German words for *mother* are essentially the same word. English *mother* is German *Mutter*. Although there is a slight difference in the pronunciation of these two words, to linguists they are essentially the same word.

When similar words are found in different languages, as in the case of the word for *mother* in German and English, there are three possible explanations for the coincidence. The similarity came about either because of **accident**, by **borrowing**, or through **shared descent**. These three possible explanations represent a standard scientific method, not unique to linguistics, known as the **comparative method**. The same method can be used when comparing sets of almost anything: disease, DNA, technology, plants. If, for example, historians learned that contemporary people of central Africa and of southern Europe both had iron technology, they could ask the comparative question: was the coincidence of iron technology an accident, was the technology borrowed from one culture to the other, or did the two inherit the technology from the same source? Linguists attempt to answer this type of question wherever they discover similar words. The answers help us trace the historical relationships between people and culture.

If the words for *mother* in German and English are the same because of accident, this would mean that there is no relationship between the two words. German-speaking people and English-speaking people would have chosen similar sounds to describe the same thing. In most cases involving similar words, however, it is highly improbable that such an accident could occur; it is very unlikely that two different cultures, while developing language, chose randomly the same set of sounds to identify the same object or action. There are millions of combinations of sounds and tens of thousands of things to name. For these combinations to accidentally agree is a remote enough possibility that the option of "accident" can ordinarily be eliminated.

If the words *mother* and *Mutter* are similar because of borrowing, this would mean that one language had the word (in this case, the word for *mother*), and when the two cultures came into contact, one people adopted the word from the other's language. Borrowing words from one language to another is very common and usually occurs when one culture has a word that does not exist in the other culture. For example, when Vikings sailed to western Europe, they brought with them a technology that was different and in some ways superior to that of the native people of the British Isles and France. Vikings simultaneously contributed to English culture a vocabulary and a technology. Perhaps the more famous story of Vikings is violence and conflict, but the transference of culture was important and enduring. English received words from Norse Vikings and, over time, from Scandinavia that represented aspects of northern life, such as *skipper*, *ski*, and *keel*.

When vocabularies are borrowed, they often carry with them the "face" of one people to another. Consider a set of words borrowed from Japanese. These words represent technologies, ideas, and features that English-speaking people received from Japanese. The words also represent an American impression of Japanese culture.

English Words and Meanings Borrowed from Japanese

> *sake*: Japanese rice wine
> *kamikaze*: divine wind, suicide dive bomber from Second World War
> *bonsai*: a type of trimmed tree
> *geisha*: a dignified and formal serving woman
> *karate*: a style of martial art
> *ninja*: a member of a secret warrior society
> *kimono*: a Japanese dress
> *hara-kiri*: ritual suicide
> *tsunami*: a tidal wave
> *samurai*: a member of a warrior society
> *soy*: a salty flavoring
> *sushi*: a fish dish

To a native Japanese this set of words might not show more than a stereotype of what is most Japanese, but to a person who encounters Japanese society through these words alone, Japanese culture might be represented by the sum of these "typical" features.

An understanding of borrowed words helps construct the historical record of the relationships between people. We can tell from the above list something about when, where, and under what circumstances Japanese speakers came into contact with English speakers. Through research using all sources, historians can reconstruct the historical relationship between Japanese people and English-speaking people.

Many thousands of new words have entered the English language in the past five hundred years, some borrowed, some created. The entire vocabularies of auto mechanics, computers, the Internet, space travel, and other fields have entered our language only since the appearance of those areas of knowledge. At the same time, other words disappear or change in meaning.

This brings us to the third explanation for coincidence in different languages: common descent. *Descent* means to descend from a common ancestor, in this case, a common ancestral language. Words can pass down through time, and as a language evolves, some words disappear, others change, and still others resist change. Words that remain in use even after languages diverge are similar because of common descent. The words descend from the same ancestor, dating to when the divergent languages were one language.

Language can change very rapidly or slowly, but it always changes. For example, we call the English language spoken by people during the time of knights and feudalism **Middle English**. Middle English was different enough from Modern English that the language of knights, lords, and peasants would hardly be recognizable to modern speakers. Even where words have remained relatively constant, pronunciations and spellings have changed. Here is the Lord's Prayer as written in Middle English by John Wycliffe in 1389.

> Oure fadir that are in heuenes
> halewid be thi name;
> thi kyngdoom cumme to;
> be thi wille don in erthe as in heuen:
> gyue to vs this dai oure breed ouer othir substaunce
> and forgyue to vs oure dettis,
> as we forgyue to oure dettouris;
> and lede vs not in to temptacioun,
> but delyuere vs fro yuel. Amen.[13]

The Lord's Prayer from a few centuries earlier would be even less recognizable to modern speakers and readers than this six-hundred-year-old form. This is because language changes over time even in the case of this text, which uses essentially the same vocabulary as the Modern English version.

English is a language from the **Indo-European** family of languages. Indo-European refers to the people, language, and culture of central Asia five or six thousand years ago. The Indo-European people were migratory, and while they held a homeland in the area of the Black Sea for many centuries, migrations took people to places distant from central Asia. Migrants brought with them Indo-European culture and language, and as they encountered new people, new languages, and new environments, the languages they brought with them changed over time. Some Indo-European people migrated to the south and east, where they evolved into one of the great

---

13. *The Lord's Prayer in Five Hundred Languages Comprising the Leading Languages and Their Principal Dialects,* preface by Reinhold Rost, CIF, LLD, PhD (London: Gilbert & Rivington, 1905), 47.1.

cultures of the world, that of the **Sanskrit**. Sanskrit language is still used today in India as a sacred language. Other Indo-European people migrated west, southwest, and northwest, and the languages and cultures of each group developed unique characteristics. Over time, Indo-European people came to dominate the European subcontinent. Today their descendants speak languages in the **Germanic**, **Celtic**, **Latin**, and **Slavic** families to name the largest.

As languages and cultures evolved, certain elements resisted change. Some religious rites, hunting habits, family organizations, and many words and phrases did not change much over hundreds and even thousands of years. Words tend to resist change when they represent fundamental, universal things such as family members, body parts, numbers, and things that are constant regardless of culture or environment. Universals such as *milk*, *finger*, *one*, and *brother* are never lost, and every culture has these things. When one culture meets another, neither needs a word for *finger*, as all people possess fingers and words to name them. And though words change in pronunciation, and if there is a written form, spelling, the shape of the word often remains intact. Linguists are able to trace many modern words to ancient Indo-European words and, despite the fact that the language was not written and has been extinct for thousands of years, have been able to reconstruct from modern vocabularies a large part of the Indo-European language.

German, English, Gaelic, Italian, Persian, Spanish, Swedish, Sanskrit, and all other Indo-European languages and cultures descended from an ancestral Indo-European. Because we use the terms of family lineage to describe relationships between languages, we name Indo-European the "ancestor" to all "descended" languages and cultures. The relationship between all contemporary languages in the Indo-European family is therefore cousin. In fact, since all languages descend from common ancestral languages and all modern languages exist in the same "generation," all modern languages are cousin languages. Some are more distant than others, but all are cousins.

Characteristics of Shared Words: The Descent of the Indo-European Words *Mead, Mater,* and *Ster*

A word can descend only from the older to the younger. (As with a physical trait, one cannot inherit a trait from one's own children or grandchildren!) A word also cannot descend between cousin languages. Using the simplified tree of Indo-European languages below, write in the box beneath a language the word as it appeared in that language. The example given in the chart below shows the word *mead* in three modern Indo-European languages and five ancestral Indo-European languages, including Proto-Indo-European, shown at the bottom of the chart. Highlight each occurrence of the word for *mead* in the eight languages. *Mead* is an alcoholic drink made from fermenting honey. It was a drink produced by Indo-European people thousands of years ago and is still available today.

Using the chart for the word *mead*, answer the following questions:

1. Is it possible the Modern English word *mead* descended from the Modern German word (*met*) for mead?

2. Is it possible the English word *mead* descended from the Proto-Indo-European word (*medhu*) for mead?

3. Is it possible the English word *mead* descended from the Sanskrit word (*madhu*) for mead?

(continued)

4. Does the Danish word *mød* share a common ancestor with the German word *met*? If so, name that ancestor.

5. Is it more likely the eight words identified as meaning *mead* are similar because of accident, borrowing, or common ancestry?

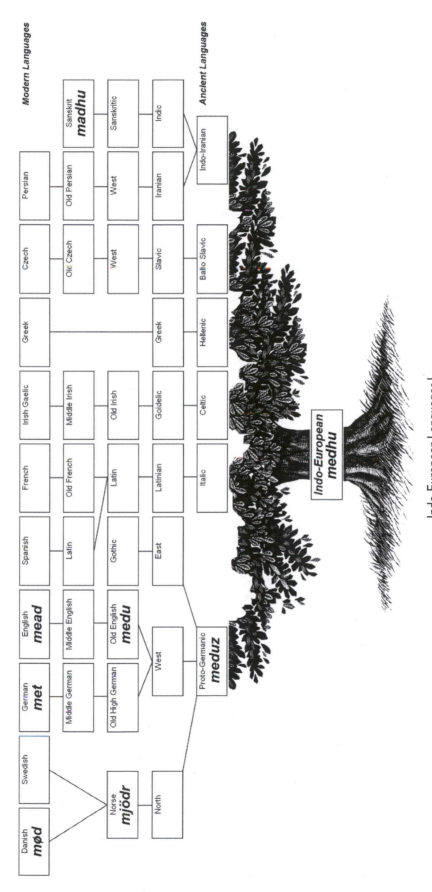

Indo-European Languages I.

A simplified family chart of Indo-European languages, showing the descent of the Indo-European word for *mead*.
Courtesy of Paul Hertzel.

PROJECT 12B
Descent of the Indo-European Word *Mater*

If we return to the German and English words for *mother*, we can reconstruct a simple genealogy of German and English by diagramming the descent of this ancient word. Show the descent of the word *mother* by writing the word for *mother* in the box beneath the appropriate language in the chart on the following page. This project provides an example of words that are similar because of shared descent. The word *Mutter* in German descended from the Indo-European word for mother, *mater*. The same is true of the word *mother* in English; it also descended from the Indo-European word *mater*.

Language: Word Meaning *Mother*

Proto-Indo-European: *mater*
Proto-Germanic: *mothaer*
Old English: *modor*
Middle English: *mother*
Modern English: mother
Modern German: *Mutter*
Latin: *mater*
Old Irish: *mathir*
Irish Gaelic: *mathir*
Sanskrit: *matar*
Greek: *meter*
Spanish: *madre*
Danish: *moder*
Swedish: *moder*
Modern Czech: *matka*
Modern French: *mère*

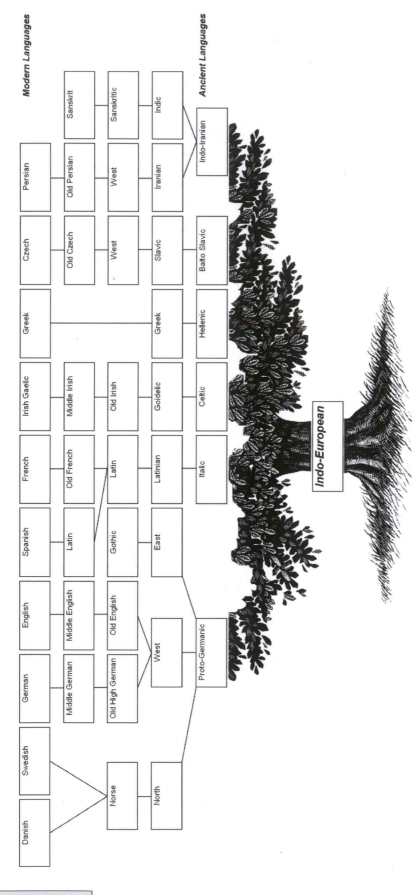

Indo-European Languages II.

A simplified family chart of Indo-European languages. Following the list given, fill in the appropriate blocks to show the descent of the Indo-European word for *mother*. Courtesy of Paul Hertzel.

Descent of the Indo-European Word *Ster*

Using the chart on the following page, show the descent of the word *star* by copying the word for *star* in the box of the corresponding language. You do not need to fill in boxes for any other languages than those listed here.

Language: Word Meaning *Star*

Proto-Indo-European: *ster*
Proto-Germanic: *sterson*
Old English: *steorra*
Middle English: *sterre*
Modern English: star
Gothic: *stairno*
Old High German: *sterro*
Modern German: *stern*
Spanish: *estrella*
Sanskrit: *star*
Swedish: *stjärna*
Latin: *stella*
Norse: *stjarna*
Danish: *stjerne*

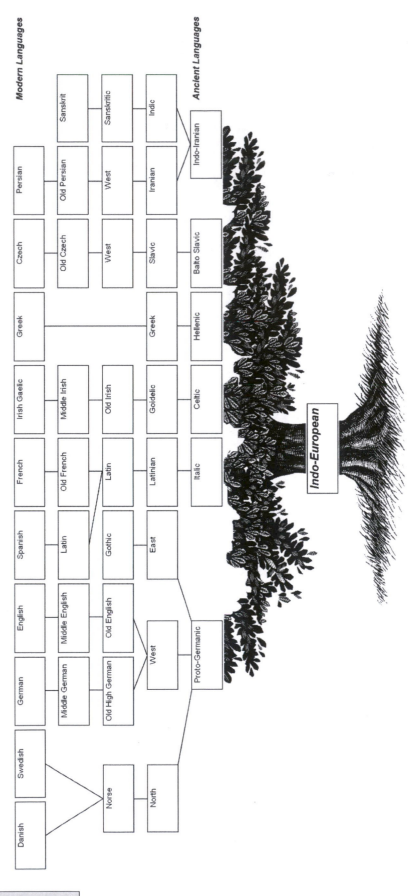

Indo-European Languages III.

A simplified family chart of Indo-European languages, showing the descent of the Indo-European word for *star*.
Courtesy of Paul Hertzel.

Borrowing Words and Adapting the Comparative Method

1. As we have seen, when one finds similarities of root words in multiple languages, this could indicate either mass borrowing or shared descent. But a word could not descend from a language that did not have the thing the word represents. Therefore, the word for *computer* could not have descended from Proto-Indo-European since the Indo-Europeans lived five thousand years ago and did not have computers. The words listed below are similar in many modern Indo-European languages. Could these words have descended from the Indo-European mother language of five thousand years ago? Write *possible* or *not possible* next to each word.

    computer

    _____

    brother

    _____

    two

    _____

    Internet

    _____

    steel

    _____

    New Jersey

    _____

    mead

    _____

    Jesus (of the New Testament)

    _____

    eye

    _____

    hunt

    _____

    father

    _____

    grass

    _____

    telephone

    _____

    moon

    _____

(continued)

2. Using the comparative method, explain the coincidence of themes, arche-types, and motifs in literature and myths throughout history and around the world. For specific examples around which to frame your answer, refer to projects 9, 10, and 11.

THE STORY OF ENGLISH

English grew out of the Germanic family of languages. After Indo-European people migrated to different regions, each group gradually incorporated local cultures and environments to develop cultures and languages independent of other Indo-Europeans. Those who were to become Germanic people lived in tribal communities, each with a distinct language, customs, and kinship organization. Tribes interacted and shared many features, but each tribe also established a unique character.

For several centuries beginning with the third century CE, large kinship or tribal groups of Germanic people migrated out from central and northern Europe into other parts of Europe and the Mediterranean world. The **Vandals** migrated through Spain into northern Africa, where they conquered local states but were eventually assimilated into the native populations. Goths split into two major groups, Visigoths and Ostrogoths, and also migrated south, the first to establish a kingdom in Spain, the other to assimilate into the native populations of southeastern Europe. Most important to the story of the development of English were the tribal migrations of the **Saxons and Angles**.

People of the Saxon tribe wandered from the central European homeland in numerous waves, including a series of migrations across the English Channel to the British Isles. These resettlements took place around the fourth and fifth centuries and coincided with migrations of Angle people to the same region. When the Saxons and Angles arrived, they encountered Celtic people who had inhabited the islands for many centuries. Eventually the culture of the Saxons and the Angles replaced the Celtic languages in the southeastern regions, and thus emerged a new language, Anglo-Saxon, also known as Old English. This language and culture dominated all aspects of life in the region and evolved as its own culture, independent of the Germanic cultures on the continent, though considerable contact continued. Over the next thousand years, many great influences and changes came to the Anglo-Saxon language and culture, particularly from Danish Vikings and in 1066 from **Normans**, invaders from the continent.

Normans were Norsemen (Northmen) who had lived long enough in the land of the Romanized Franks (modern France) that their old language had evolved into a language with a Latin base, called *French Norman*. When the Normans conquered Anglo-Saxon territory, they implemented French Norman as the language of administration. The new language thus entered English first as a language of foreign rule, but eventually its influence and use migrated into everyday speech. By the fourteenth century, English had become a language that was truly an amalgamation of different Indo-European languages: Celtic, Angle, Saxon, Danish, and Norman French. Because English was a melting pot of many different languages, it still has one of the largest vocabularies of any language in the world.

As much as people frequently define themselves by distinguishing cultural differences, it should be evident from the story of English that the formation of culture is a historical process of exchange and intersection, or borrowing and descending (and rarely accident). Exchange and intersection are perpetual in human history and occur through contact and inheritance. No people are long isolated, and no culture is wholly original. People and languages disappear, while new ones emerge, but not from thin air. Every culture is unique, but, like individuals, is also a descendant and a relative. Indo-European languages are cousins, but so are all languages cousins. For while English, Spanish, Russian, Sanskrit, and hundreds more languages descended from Indo-European, all languages ever spoken descended from the First Language.

PROJECT 14
Inherited Culture

Identify words and features of American life that are inherited from non-English-speaking or non-American cultures.

1. Foods: Name five dishes with non-English names, for example, pizza from Italian.

2. Music: Name three songs that come from non-American groups or traditions, for example, "Danny Boy" from Irish.

3. Corporations: Name three corporations with non-American headquarters and manufacturing, for example, Olivetti, Italy, printers.

4. Places: Name five place names that have become standard American English but that come from non-English words, for example, Los Angeles, from Spanish; Bismarck, from German.

5. Name four common words in English that do not fit the categories listed above but that represent actions, things, or mentalities and originate from a language other than English, for example, chauffeur, from French.

CHAPTER 3

Contrasting Concepts in Religious Traditions

A S MUCH AS civilizations and people share ancestries and DNA, myths and ideas, and aspects of culture, historical contrasts among societies are also not difficult to find. Religious traditions can provide powerful and concrete historical examples of both human universals and contrasting principles. There are shared principles fundamental to all religions while there are also great differences of interpretation between religious teachings on themes such as the role of women in a public sphere, family structure, reason, justice, and law, the afterlife, and the nature of God. Even within singular religious traditions, over time there can be great contrasts in interpretations. Sometimes religions that are closely related can be the most contentious, as in the case of periodic European wars of religion that set Catholic against Protestant states. But all religious traditions share some elements and differ on others.

Judaism, Christianity, and Islam are historically and theologically closely related and originate from common sources. All three are monotheistic. All three claim Abraham as a patriarch, and all three claim particular prophets as part of their theological and cultural genealogies. All three recognize particular texts as sacred and depend heavily on historical events for their identities. Yet these three religions also contrast in many ways, sometimes perceived by believers to be great enough to render the other blasphemy. Christianity and **Islam** have records of stark contrasts and conflict. Yet historically, these two religions are closely related and descend from common traditions. Both recognize the Hebrew tradition as a religious and spiritual forerunner (naming Abraham in particular as a patriarch and recognizing Moses as a prophet, for example); both acknowledge concepts of equality before God among believers; both recognize a written text as sacred; both depend heavily on historical figures; and both endorse certain methods—sometimes aggressive methods—of conversion. But there are differences as well. The precise message and the spiritual nature of the respective messenger of the two religions are different; while Islam proclaims **Muhammad**, the seventh-century prophet of Islam, to be a man summoned by God to be a prophet, Christians proclaim Jesus to be the Christ, the son of God, and a personal redeemer. The sacred texts are different as well. While Muslims believe the sacred text of Islam, the **Qur'an** (Koran, Q'ran), came to Muhammad in a series of revelations from God, Christians accept a tradition of selection, translation, and recording, including the Hebrew sacred texts, to arrive at a collection of divine writings coming from many centuries and different languages. The Qur'an also accepts the basic truth of the Hebrew tradition but does not include the Hebrew texts as part of its own.

Islam recognizes two major texts as sacred. The first, and the text on which Islam was initially founded, is the Qur'an, which is taught to be the word of God (Allah) delivered to Muhammad, the Messenger of God, from angels. The second is the **Sunnah**, an account of Muhammad's life, recorded by contemporaries to provide the life of Muhammad as a model for all Muslims to follow. The Sunnah provides details of the teaching of Muhammad, usually through the example of his life. The daily problems and special circumstances are commonly related through stories such as this account of a woman who asks Muhammad whether she might be allowed to meet her father's pilgrimage obligation in his place.

> The woman said, "O Allah's Apostle! The obligation of Hajj [pilgrimage] enjoined by Allah on His devotees has become due on my father and he is old and weak, and he cannot sit firm on the Mount; may I perform Hajj on his behalf?" The Prophet replied, "Yes, you may." That happened during the Hajj-al-Wida (of the Prophet).[1]

In a second passage from the Sunnah, Muhammad describes the way he receives visions.

> Narrated 'Aisha (the mother of the faithful believers): Al-Harith bin Hisham asked Allah's Apostle, "O Allah's Messenger! How is the Divine Inspiration revealed to you?" Allah's Apostle replied, "Sometimes it is (revealed) like the ringing of a bell, this form of Revelation is the hardest of all and then this state passes off after I have grasped what is revealed. Sometimes the Angel comes in the form of a man and talks to me and I grasp whatever he says." 'Aisha added: Verily I saw the Prophet being inspired (Divinely) and noticed the Sweat

---

1. *The Translation of the Meaning of Sahih Al-Bukhari*, volume 2, book 26, number 589, trans. Dr. Muhammad Muhsin Khan (Medina, Saudi Arabia: Islamic University, 1976), 344.

dropping from his forehead on a very cold day (as the Revelation was over).[2]

These passages show Muhammad's humanity in the way he discusses issues with people who come to him. One of Muhammad's messages was the equality of all people. The Sunnah also provides specific doctrine, again through the voice of the Prophet of Islam. In some passages Muhammad outlines the foundation of the religion and describes the "end days," another theme Islam shares with Christianity.

The Qur'an is different from the Sunnah; it is taught as the word of God, and its voice is God speaking to humanity. The images of God and the religious teachings in the two texts are thematically consistent, but the tones are different. Here is one passage where God (Allah) explains the difference between legalistic righteousness and true righteousness.

It is not righteousness that you turn your faces towards the East and the West, but righteousness is this that one should believe in Allah and the last day and the angels and the Book and the prophets, and give away wealth out of love for Him to the near of kin and the orphans and the needy and the wayfarer and the beggars and for (the emancipation of) the captives, and keep up prayer and pay the poor-rate; and the performers of their promise when they make a promise, and the patient in distress and affliction and in time of conflicts—these are they who are true (to themselves) and these are they who guard (against evil).[3]

2. *The Translation of the Meaning of Sahih Al-Bukhari*, volume 1, book 1, number 2, trans. Dr. Muhammad Muhsin Khan (Medina, Saudi Arabia: Islamic University, 1997), 46.

3. Chapter 2, Sura Al-Baqurah, verse 177, in *The Holy Qur'an*, trans. M. H. Shakir (Mountain View, CA: Wiretap, 1990s).

PROJECT 15
What the Qur'an Says about Jesus

There is an interesting historical-religious relationship between Islam and Christianity. Search the Qur'an online or in a bound volume that has an index (use the library!) to find a passage that describes a view of Jesus. Many searchable texts are available online for your use. Search until you find a single, understandable passage (like all sacred texts, if you are not familiar with the religion, it can be difficult to understand), and then summarize the text in your own words, copy the exact wording of the text, and cite the chapter and verse of the passage you used.

1. Cite the Qur'an passage (sura or chapter name, chapter number, and verse number).

2. Quote the Qur'an passage.

3. Summarize the Qur'an passage.

To study religion historically means to avoid judgments of "correct" or "incorrect" in order to critically (objectively) evaluate the impact of religion on history. Historians define religious practice and traditions in terms of what the practices are and not what they "should be." Discussions of the historical Christ therefore refer to the verifiable person rather than the object of faith. The same is true of historical Muhammad or historical Buddha; these refer to the person about whom events can be confirmed objectively (as with any historical person, George Washington, Martin Luther King, or Confucius).

Ancient Greek scholars of the classical era sought to guide religious inquiry with objectivity and reason. In one famous dialogue, Socrates, one of the great philosophers of the ancient world, instructs Meno on the nature of good and evil from a rational perspective. When reading this Socratic excerpt (appendix 1), consider Socrates's method and message, both of which are based on reason. This "rational" approach also extended to matters of morality and the nature of God.

As religious traditions vary from society to society, so within a historical tradition religious interpretations change over time. Christian practice does not appear the same in one century as it does in the next. While internal or spiritual constants may define spirituality, external practice adopts new forms and abandons old definitions and practices, and doctrines and teachings adapt to new environments and new learning. The modern scientific method has, for example, eliminated many older remnants of pre-Christian practice still common during the ancient and medieval eras in Europe.

Thus we see religious practice, like language and other aspects of human civilization, is fluid and adaptable. In the modernizing world, as people came to accept Galileo's scientific description of our solar system, for example, interpretations of the Bible changed to incorporate new learning and discoveries. In fact, the religion of the premodern Christian church might be barely recognizable today. Consider a twelve-hundred-year-old blessing, performed by Anglo-Saxon Christians (appendix 2). The Anglo-Saxons believed in the living body of **Mother Earth** and an organic relationship of all things spiritual and physical. Modern Christians might not recognize this ritual; there is no precise scriptural outline, and the blessing comes from a distant time and place. It might appear "superstitious" as well, as it draws from a nonscientific understanding of fertility and agriculture. Yet to the Anglo-Saxon people who practiced it, the blessing was part of Christian agricultural life.

PROJECT 16
Interpreting an Anglo-Saxon Blessing of the Fields

1. Modern science functions from the premise that all physical phenomena have physical causes. What elements from the text of the blessing show the Anglo-Saxon Blessing (appendix 2) to be prescientific?

2. What specific elements or terms appear in the blessing that identify practitioners as Christian?

3. How does the Anglo-Saxon Blessing demonstrate that over time a religious tradition changes?

4. Read the selection from the Hymns of Homer in appendix 22. The text was written in the Mediterranean world a thousand years before the Anglo-Saxon blessing. Which characteristics does the Homeric hymn share with the Anglo-Saxon blessing? (Use passages from the Hymns of Homer to support your answer.) How can you explain this coincidence? Does accident, borrowing, or common ancestry appear to make more sense?

In contrast to Christianity, Islam, and Judaism, the traditional religious practice of the **Zulu** presents a religion without a written tradition and one that includes spiritual elements absent in the others. While there are Zulu who practice other religions, including Islam and Christianity, the traditional and most ancient practice of the Zulu can be described as **animism**. Animism is one of humanity's original and most persistent religious teachings. The basic belief of animism is contained in the word, which comes from the Latin *anima*, meaning "soul," and describes something alive, as in the verb *to animate*. Animism is the belief that all things have spiritual life; trees, animals, plants, rocks, the moon, dust, all things are part of a spiritual universe that lies behind the physical world, and all things have souls.

The stories in appendix 6 representing Zulu life are not necessarily religious texts. Yet both *Amatongo* and *The Healing Spirits of the Zulu* describe religious thinking and practice, or both reveal the spiritual understanding of the Zulu's universe. Both accounts deal with life and death, ancestral spirits, healing practices, spiritual guidance, and, in a sense, "worship." Although the texts do not refer to an all-powerful, creating God, neither do they deny such a God. By most accounts, the Zulu believed in the existence of a supreme God, but their daily routine was remote from God; instead, Zulu religious practice involved more immediate spiritual relationships, as shown in both stories.

The mystery of James, the sick young man in the story *Amatongo*, is his illness. It was his mystery as well as ours when we read this account today. The witnesses are friends of his, Christians from a village where James has lived for some time with his wife and children. But James's sickness has destroyed apparently everything. He despises his home, his village, his religion, even his family. Initially, it might appear James is simply rejecting his adopted religion, Christianity, to return to his native Zulu beliefs. But his disease is less discriminating than that. His symptoms seem bizarre and capricious. One key to understanding James's sickness is the fact that doctors among the Zulu use spiritual as well as physical causes to explain physical conditions. James is aware that the European-trained doctors of his village would simply have him committed to an asylum were he to ask for diagnosis.

The anthropologist Mircea Eliade and the historian Howard Spodek have identified several features shared by all religious traditions. The list includes *sacred time*, including holidays; *sacred space*, including cities, altars, graves, and so on; *sacred languages and literature*, including traditions written or oral; *sacred artistic and cultural creativity*, including paintings, architecture, colors, dress, music, and so on; *the creation of religious organization*, which might include any authority from the local to the heavenly; and *the sanctification of predecessors*, including saints, martyrs, and kinship groups, including families. Such categories are useful to historians as objective criteria for identification and comparison of religious practice and can be located in the texts we have been studying.

PROJECT 17
Comparative Religions: Islam, Animism of the Zulu, and the Christianity of the Anglo-Saxons

Identify features from the religious texts identified below. Use quotations and explain briefly how your examples fit the categories. Use complete sentences.

1. How might James's symptoms lead him to become a **diviner**? In particular, why might he need to reject his family, his religion, his village, and his friends in order to practice as a traditional diviner?

2. In *The Healing Spirits of the Zulu*, the narrator reports, "We worshipped our ancestors," yet the father of the sick child refers to the ancestral spirits as "fools." What might the narrator mean by "worship"?

3. Writing in complete sentences, explain how the two Zulu stories can be used as examples of animism.

4. How and why must the Zulu diviner learn about natural features, landscapes, and animals? In what way is this belief "animist"?

MYSTIC TRADITIONS WORLDWIDE

There are universals in world religions that go beyond the categories of comparison identified in project 17. In contrast to the literary theme of "the pain of separation" is a religious theme, "the union of all things," what the Jewish mystic Abraham Isaak Kook describes as "all beings longing for the source of their origin."[4] In *On Prayer*, Rabbi Kook writes,

> All beings long for the very source of their origin. Every plant, every grain of sand, every lump of earth, small creatures and big ones, the heavens above and the angels, every substance together with its particles—all of them are longing, yearning, panting to attain the state of holy perfection. Man suffers all the time from this homesickness of the soul and it is in prayer that he cures it. When praying, man feels at one with the whole creation and he raises it to the very source of blessing and life.[5]

In most religious traditions, similar themes are expressed through **mystical practices**.

Evelyn Underhill describes the aim of mysticism as the "union between God and the soul." One can find mystical thinking in every religious practice. Some traditions, such as **Buddhism** and some Native American religions, might be defined as mysticism rather than as religions. Islam has a mystic tradition called **Sufism**. Christianity has had many mystic traditions throughout its history, commonly following the precedent set by Jesus' example of prayer, fasting, and meditation, and his message of the spiritual "kingdom of God."[6] Judaism contains mystical traditions, texts, and prayers, including the collection known as the *Kabbalah*. In Confucian traditions, the teaching of the Tao and its various historical additions begins with the potential of humans to find harmony with the universal divine, also a mystical theme. And the animism of the Zulu includes the communion of all things living and not living, a common aspect of mysticism. Even modern science has contributed to the mystic discussion with recent research in neurology and the brain supporting an argument that humans have an innate spirituality that can be awakened by meditation and ritual, the typical practices of mysticism. Thus, while we find many interpretations of religion, we also find in mysticism a commonality of basic spiritual belief.

Mysticism shuns doctrine and it commonly describes truth as more of a mystery than a law. In the ancient Buddhist text *The Diamond Sutra*, the teacher declares, "If anyone set forth a teaching he really slanders Buddha

---

4. Cited in *Modern Jewish Thought: A Source Reader*, ed. Nahum N. Glatzer (New York: Schocken Books, 1977), 71.
5. *Modern Jewish Thought*, 71.
6. For example, see Luke 17:21 and I Corinthians 15:50.

and is unable to explain what I teach. As to any truth-declaring system, truth is undeclarable; so, 'an enunciation of truth' is just the name given to it."[7] This passage expresses well how mysticism defies category because mystics seek an internal person not shaped by culture and man-made systems. Because its intent is inherently universal, mysticism can be used to explore patterns of belief that underlie world religions.

ANCESTORS

Honoring one's ancestors is an important or even a central element to many cultural and religious traditions. Through death, ancestors might become part of a sacred order of the universe and serve as contacts of the living to the worlds of the dead. Ancestors are honored as sacred (not to say divine) in practices of the Zulu, in Muhammad's instruction to the young woman regarding the Hajj and her father, in God's promise to Abraham, in the Christian account of the life of Jesus, in filial practices in modern Korea and Taiwan, and in many other traditions throughout history and across the world. In short, "Honor thy Father and thy Mother" is a universal command, present in all religious traditions and many secular ones as well.

The types of practices involving "honoring" ancestors ranges from simple funeral rites or prayers *for the dead* to elaborate sacrifices and rituals and prayers *to the dead*. Some societies structure entire hierarchies of authority, ownership of property, and other laws around family lineage. Others, such as members of the Church of Jesus Christ of Latter Day Saints (Mormons), teach that families are sacred organizations that will be together after this life. In short, many societies consider ancestry and family to be a natural order ordained by God.

Christianity awards special attention to the significance of ancestry in the Gospel according to Matthew, which outlines the genealogy of Jesus as part of the fulfillment of divine prophecy. In Judaism, family and ancestry hold divine associations, such as marking the lineages of Kohan. In the book of Genesis, God promises to Abraham, "And I will make thy seed as the dust of the earth: so that if a man can number the dust of the earth, then shall thy seed also be numbered" (King James translation, Genesis 13:16). Hindus and Buddhists perform numerous ceremonies on behalf of the dead. Honoring the spirits of the dead is common across Asia today. In short, along with animism and mysticism, honoring ancestors can be described as a religious and cultural universal.

---

7. A. F. Price and Wong Mou-Lam, *The Diamond Sutra and The Sutra of Hui-Neng* (Boston: Shambala, 1990), 42.

CHAPTER 4

Confucianism and Humanism

O VER TIME, societies develop grand principles of the self and society to explain and justify traditions, institutions, and practices. People become so accustomed to the principles of their own societies that they often come to believe their principles are part of natural or divine orders. One system of principles so deeply ingrained in the mentalities of American and European societies is the tradition of **humanism**, that set of ideals that conventionally define the **Western tradition** and that serve as a foundation to much of modern institutional life. Humanism is so deeply integrated into modern perceptions, many people take this grand intellectual tradition for granted. Yet humanism is not universally practiced.

Humanism refers to a trust in human reason, the scientific method, and individual liberty and equality. Most societies with humanist traditions, including the United States, Japan, much of Latin America, Europe, Canada, and so on, accept reason, liberty, and equality as "natural" guiding ideals on which to build law and society, though there are historically many variations on these basic principles. The major documents and developments of American political history are humanist, at least in intent. The Declaration of Independence, for example, is humanist in its claim to **freedom** of the individual.

Humanism is a guiding principle and a way of understanding the "self" and the universe. There are humanist Christians, atheists, Hindus, socialists, libertarians, Republicans, and people from most any religious belief or political ideology. Humanism is not a specific ideology in any narrow sense, although it would be difficult for a fascist or any person who rejects the use of reason to claim humanism.

Many societies in history have held and practiced various concepts of humanist freedom. It is to the Athenians of classical Greece, however, that the European humanist tradition conventionally looks for an "original" model. The ancient Greeks taught that man is a heroic creature who is able to challenge the gods to seize his own fate and that if he does not follow his own rational reason, he becomes the victim of his fate. Greeks believed that a man holds tremendous power to define his own life if he will have courage and seize opportunity, but he needs to be educated so as to not be led astray by self-serving entities, such as kings or religious leaders.

Working from a concept of the noble individual, Greeks established the institution of the individual **citizen** who has the authority to build his own society and govern himself. The Greek citizen owned a natural right and responsibility, not so much to his family, the king, or the gods, but rather to his own personal conscience. The result of the institution of the free citizen ideally would benefit the common good, for smart, respected citizens would return their accomplishments to the society that enabled them and to which they, as citizens, contributed. This concept of the citizen departed from previous (and also later) societies that assigned authority not to citizens as such but only to people of privilege, kings, or those who ruled by "divine right." Greek humanism strove to remove privilege from aristocratic classes and install a more democratic system. Every freeborn male Greek citizen had the right to participate in the political process, to deliberately contribute to the construction of laws, traditions, and social institutions. Because of the peculiar tradition of the heroic free individual, it has become conventional, though still controversial, to name Athens the ancestor to modern democracies.

PROJECT 18
Socrates and Humanism

Read the dialogue between Socrates and Meno in appendix 1. The humanism of Socrates in this passage lies as much in his method as in his argument. Describe in your own words the method Socrates uses in the dialogue. Then answer the question: In what way is the Socratic method humanist?

There were more slaves than freeborn males in most of the city-states of classical Greece, and women did not participate in public institutional life. In fact, only freeborn males held the rights of citizenship. While this plainly was not a democratic society, it was a society that established an ideal of rule by committee rather than by privileged individual. When an individual is granted complete authority, the possibility always exists of decisions based on personal issues, whim, emotion, revenge, or poor judgment. A collective decision, when made without regard to status, is expected to be more balanced, more **inclusive**, and more reasonable simply by virtue of the greater perspective it includes.

The tradition of humanism has dominated political and social understanding in European societies for more than two hundred years, but the record is not absolute. Within and among humanist societies, there are differing interpretations of freedom, the individual, and the use of reason. Censorship is greater in one European society than in another, freedom of speech is stronger in some European societies than in the United States, and one society interprets the role of women differently from another. Furthermore, within single national traditions there have been different interpretations of humanism from one era to the next. Germany in the twenty-first century has one of the world's most **egalitarian** societies and has been a major contributor to every phase of humanism since the sixteenth century. Yet in the 1930s in Germany, fascist parties that opposed democracy, freedom, and the use of reason abolished the rule of law and came to power with the support of a large section of the German electorate, though not a majority. Clearly the historical record in Germany has been mixed. The pattern has been equally uneven in other national examples. Yet overall, more than any other single feature, European and American societies share the pursuit of humanist ideals.

PROJECT 19
Inclusion, Democracy, Athens, and Women

1. Why can inclusion in the public process be used as a measurement of democracy?

2. Is it humanist to include women in the public process (i.e., politics, education, workforce, etc.)?

3. Measure the degree to which the United States is a democratic society. How do you measure this? Is there a difference between the law and the practice of inclusion? (Explain this answer.)

4. How democratic was ancient Athens?

In Chinese civilizations, humanist ideals have not often prevailed. Instead, if there is a dominant set of cultural and political traditions around which to define Chinese civilizations, it would be the teachings of **Confucius** and the Tao. These two principles have worked to define the foundations of Chinese traditions far longer than the traditions of humanism have defined "the West," and Confucian influence covers much of the rest of Asia as well. Chinese society has applied the two guiding principles continuously, if somewhat unevenly, for more than twenty-five centuries. As with the West, Confucian and Taoist traditions have been interpreted differently from century to century but overall have survived and are still central to Chinese thinking today.

Confucianism grew out of teachings of Confucius, while the Taoist tradition emerged over time from a collection of writings attributed to the (probably legendary) Lao-tzu. The two schools are complementary but deal with different aspects of life and society. The Tao (or Dao) refers to a path leading to spiritual harmony with all things related as female and male, dark and light, yin and yang. Balancing these elements leads to a mystical sense of internal harmony of the person with the universe. Since the Tao seeks to balance all things, the teaching might include political teaching as well as spiritual, but according to the Tao, true harmony cannot be gained by building a better society. Harmony is attained internally when one understands and accepts the harmony of a universal, divine order. In Tao, human beings do not create or establish paths to harmony; it is instead for people to accept their proper positions in "the natural state" of things. It is for people to listen and understand. The principal text of Tao teaching is the Tao Te Ching.

Confucian teaching has been interpreted and reinterpreted for more than two thousand years but has always been based on the teachings of Confucius, a Chinese civil servant who lived five hundred years before Christ. The principal texts of the Confucian tradition are the Analects of Confucius, the Doctrine of the Mean, and the Mandate of Heaven. Confucius taught that the ancient ancestors held a more pure understanding of correct behavior that should always correspond to the underlying nature of the universe. But unlike Taoism, Confucianism deals with external behavior more than with personal, internal development.

Confucianism maintains that every person, like every creature in the universe, has a specific nature that brings it into accord with a universal order. If one deviates from one's nature, he deviates from the inherent truth that defines him, and order begins to collapse. Each person therefore carries a responsibility not according to his own choice but according to his nature. In Confucian tradition, a person does not defy his fate, as with the Greeks. On the contrary, each person embraces his or her fate to make the most of it.

Confucian teaching has direct application in the social and political spheres; it is not overtly religious and addresses the external person more than the internal person. It is less "religious" than the writings of the Tao. Confucianism admonishes rulers to behave well and for superiors to treat subordinates fairly. Confucianism seeks harmony, as does Taoism, but the former seeks external harmony first, while the latter seeks internal harmony. But harmony brings greater harmony in both teachings, and the path to a harmonious society, government, and world begins with individual responsibility or duty to follow the right path.

The contrast between Confucianism and humanism should be apparent. Whereas the former directs an individual to comply with a natural order of things, the latter encourages the individual to define the order and his place within it. There is little encouragement of the "heroic" individual in Confucian teaching, and there is little promotion of a "natural harmony" in humanism except to say that humans are born free. While there might be a concept of free will in Confucianism, individuals are not free to forge their own paths. The path is laid out; it is up to the individual to accept it or not.

PROJECT 20
Comparing Traditions: Asia and Europe

Comparing the documents representing Confucianism (appendix 11) to the humanist ideals and texts, answer the following questions:

1. The Mandate of Heaven of Confucianism refers to "heaven" as the source of the mandate. Historically, it has been common for humanist texts to appeal also to divine authority, whether named as "God," "Supreme Being," or "Creator." The American Declaration of Independence states, "We hold these truths to be self-evident, that all men are created equal, that they are endowed by their Creator with certain unalienable rights," and the French Declaration of the Rights of Man and of the Citizen claims its authority "in the auspices of the Supreme Being." Why do you suppose a divine association is common with these legal texts?

2. According to Confucianism, each animal and every person has a correct "nature" to be followed. Is there any suggestion of a human nature in the Declaration of the Rights of Man and of the Citizen? (Quote from the document.)

3. How do the Confucian texts link the common good to the Confucian principles?

(continued)

4. If Confucian principles were established as a guide toward harmony, what does *harmony* mean, and how is it achieved? What does benevolence have to do with harmony? (Write on the back of this page if necessary.)

CHAPTER 5

Humanism Comes to Define the "Western" Identity, 1500–1900

THE ANCIENT concept of humanism can be summarized in the phrase "man is the measure of all things." For the ancient Greeks, a humanist acts on the basis of reason rather than on blind trust in traditions, institutions, leaders, religious teachings, or people with titles. Greeks believed men can govern themselves using reason and therefore possess the potential of sound judgment to construct better lives and better societies. It is not an acceptable position in a humanist society to say, "We must have these laws because this is the will of the gods," or "because it has always been done this way," or "because the ruler says this is better." Rather, each individual must be free from coercive institutions and leaders to gauge for himself right and wrong, deliberate publicly and freely, and arrive at a measured, majority decision that benefits the community.

Greeks limited public participation to those deemed capable of reason: freeborn men with Greek-speaking backgrounds. No non-Greek, they supposed, was capable of reason, for outside the Greek education and experience all were barbarians. Greeks did not restrict participation on the basis of skin color but instead on culture and gender. Women did not hold the rights of citizens and never participated in public life, including institutional education. One later observer wrote that Greek philosophers believed that were it not for women, men could commune among the gods.

Humanist freedom was only partially passed along to the Greeks' western heirs, the Romans. Most notably, Roman society retained for many years the institution of citizenship. The humanist concepts of reason and the scientific method survived principally in Persia and the Islamic east. But for a thousand years after the collapse of the empire of Rome, civilization in the western regions of Europe advanced largely devoid of humanist principles. However, during the fifteenth century in the Italian city-state of Florence, there emerged among artists and scholars a revival of interest in ancient

Greek literature and art and with that a renaissance of the Greek ideal of the **heroic man**. The Renaissance humanist ideal can be seen in the grand features, posture, and attitude of Michelangelo's *David* as well as other great works of art from early modern Italy.

What began as an art movement eventually carried humanism to all spheres of activity in European cultures. Many of the great modern intellectual developments in European civilization have roots in modern humanism traced back to the Italian Renaissance. The impressive list conventionally includes a series of "revolutions" that span five hundred years and include the **Renaissance**, the **Protestant Reformation**, the **Scientific Revolution**, the **Enlightenment**, and the **French Revolution**. Respectively, these five developments reflect humanism in the spheres of art, theology, science, society, and politics. At the same time, we should be cautious to not imply that humanists of the Renaissance, Reformation, and Scientific Revolution advocated a twenty-first-century style of political freedom or equality. Humanist ideals evolved over time, sometimes slowly and incrementally, and humanist leaders of early modern Europe accepted gender and class divisions that enlightened people might today find alarming.

Far from the secular movement some modern critics describe, the humanism of the Renaissance placed man in relation to God in the universe, not apart from God. As Richard Hooker writes, "The Humanists, rather than focusing on what they considered futile questions of logic, semantics and proposition analysis, focused on the relation of the human to the divine, seeing in human beings the summit and purpose of God's creation."[1]

One of the great humanists of the Renaissance was **Giovanni Pico della Mirandola**. Pico articulated in words what Michelangelo articulated in stone: the humanist image of the heroic individual. In his essay "Oration on the Dignity of Man," Pico uses God's voice to admonish humanity to seize its own destiny and power to do good, to build rather than destroy.

> Thou, constrained by no limits, in accordance with thine own free will, in whose hand We have placed thee, shalt ordain for thyself the limits of thy nature. . . . We have made thee neither of heaven nor of earth, neither mortal nor immortal, so that with freedom of choice and with honor, as though the maker and molder of thyself, thou mayest fashion thyself in whatever shape thou shalt prefer. Thou shalt have the power to degenerate into the lower forms of life, which are brutish. Thou shalt have the power, out of thy soul's judgement, to be reborn into the higher forms, which are divine.[2]

1. Richard Hooker, *Early Modern Italian Renaissance, Pico Della Mirandola*, accessed December 2015, http://richard-hooker.com/sites/worldcultures/REN/PICO.HTM.

2. Giovanni Pico della Mirandola, "Oration on the Dignity of Man," trans. Elizabeth L. Forbes, in *The Renaissance Philosophy of Man*, ed. Ernst Cassirer, Paul Oskar Kristeller, and John H. Randall Jr. (Chicago: University of Chicago Press, 1948), 223.

The Italian Renaissance was but the first of the modern humanist movements that built the world in which we live today. But it set the tone and the terms for the revolutions to follow and in many ways became the new patriarch of humanism, replacing the dubious models from the ancient world.

If Renaissance leaders applied humanism to art and philosophy, **Martin Luther** and the leaders of the Reformations of the sixteenth century applied humanism to religion and theology. Although there were many Catholic humanist reformers, such as Erasmus, and Protestant reformers, such as John Calvin, the most influential Reformation leader was Martin Luther. The English Reformation also bears mentioning, but while politically influential, it was initially less important as part of the humanist narrative, although the churches that emerged from the English Reformation are squarely in the humanist camp today.

The Christian church based in Rome had disputed, debated, and reformed many times during its fourteen-hundred-year history before the Protestant Reformation. Saxon Martin Luther distinguished himself from those previous reforms by establishing an alternative Christian church, which divided western Christendom for the first time into two major camps, Catholic and Protestant. Luther would have preferred to reform his church rather than leave it, but the conflict between reformer and church leaders became so intense and so public that neither side was able to compromise. In short, Luther demanded that the Roman church abandon its long tradition of hierarchical organization and of council and **papal** authority over doctrine. This would have been a difficult reform for such an entrenched institution in any circumstance but was particularly difficult for the sixteenth-century Roman church, deeply involved as it was in secular political, economic, and diplomatic affairs.

Martin Luther's challenges to Roman authority began around 1519, and within ten years, the Protestant church already represented a successful, practicing alternative institution in the greater parts of northern and Germanic Europe. In the south and east of Europe, meanwhile, the Protestants lost momentum in the face of Catholic reforms that paralleled Luther's, particularly in matters of faith and education. Spain, Italy, and southern France, as well as much of the western Slavic regions, therefore remained or returned to Roman Catholicism.

The rapid success of Luther's movement can be explained in part by the fact that his major teachings—the freedom of a Christian to individually approach God without church intercession and a "literal" (scientific) interpretation of sacred scripture—were both endorsed by an already thriving humanist movement. Luther's greater success in Germanic Europe can also be explained by a growing resentment in the north toward the dominance of the Latin south and the flow of German wealth south to Rome. Luther's humanism rested on all of these aspects of his reforms: his attitude toward church hierarchy, church authority, and church traditions; his trust in his own reason and conscience; his individuality; and his scientific method in reading scriptures. Humanism had existed before Luther's time, but the Saxon applied humanism to new problems in new ways.

Luther insisted throughout his public disputes that he trusted his reason because it came as the result of study and hard work. Luther was an untiring researcher and writer, but he understood that not all people have the time and resources to study the scriptures in Latin and Greek. Luther therefore translated the Bible into his native Saxon language for his fellow Saxons to read and discern each for himself. This translation was an eminently humanist work. Luther wrote that in order for people to understand the Christian truth, they need to read for themselves the sacred scriptures and not simply accept blindly what the priest and the church proclaim. Each person must individually encounter God without the church acting as intercessor. In these things, Luther was a product of his time and intellectually indebted to the humanist teaching that spread from Renaissance Italy.

The success of the teaching that human reason can interpret scripture led to the next episode in the chronology of modern humanism, the Scientific Revolution. This movement is not as simple as the Renaissance or the Reformation to define in national or individual terms. Important contributions to the Scientific Revolution emerged in England, Poland, Italy, Scotland, and Germany. One geographic constant to the Scientific Revolution is that where the movement was welcomed, even encouraged in Protestant states, adherents in the Catholic world were persecuted and censured by a conservative church hierarchy. Great minds of the Scientific Revolution, such as Copernicus, Isaac Newton, Descartes, and **Galileo**, each contributed to a changing understanding of the physical universe. These scientists introduced laws and theories, rewriting the way we understand the world around us. But probably more important in the long run was the method they used and shared, the scientific method.

The **scientific method** is a humanist way of inquiring. Rather than believe on faith what one has been told about the way things work, the humanist scientist demands concrete testing and results. Jacob Bronowski writes that the scientific method can be summarized in three steps: build the apparatus, conduct the experiment, and publish the results.[3] This method ensures objectivity and accountability; it does not accept anything on blind faith. By *apparatus*, Bronowski refers to any measuring device that can observe something without prejudice. A ruler is an objective apparatus. Under constant conditions, a ruler measures a distance the same every time; it measures objectively, without judgment or perceptions of "big," "long," "short," and so on. It measures in units that are constant and objective.

---

3. Jacob Bronowski, *The Ascent of Man* (Boston: Little, Brown, 1974), 204.

Galileo's scientific method can be seen in his inquiry into the motion and arrangement of the solar system. Galileo built a telescope (the apparatus) with which he observed repeatedly the motions of the planets and the sun (conducted the experiment) until he was confident of the reliability of the observation. Then he published his results: the earth revolves around the sun, and the sun does not revolve around the earth.

Galileo described his findings in 1610 in a book he titled *The Starry Messenger*. The Catholic Church banned the work, which was subsequently published in Protestant countries. Rome objected to Galileo's findings because the church found them to be contrary to church teaching. Traditional church doctrine taught that regardless of what Galileo's observations suggested, the Bible makes it clear the universe revolves around the earth. The church was not interested in a humanist, scientific method in this case; it had its traditions, faith, and scripture and its rulings from councils, theologians, and religious scholars to interpret the universe. Within the church, the scientific method held little influence.

The indictment of 1633 declared Galileo's doctrine false because "the sun is immovable in the center of the world, and that the earth moves, and also with a diurnal motion." The Roman church based its position in part on scriptures such as the passage from Joshua 10:13 that states, "Move not, O sun, toward Gabaon, nor thou, O moon, toward the valley of Ajalon," whereupon "the sun and the moon stood still, till the people revenged themselves of their enemies." The first chapter of Ecclesiastes also says, "The sun riseth and goeth down and returneth to his place: and there rising again, maketh his round by the south and turneth again to the north." Other scriptures describe the "foundations of the earth," and Psalms 104 is explicit that those foundations "should not be removed forever." According to church interpretation, Galileo's scientific conclusions contradicted these and other passages.

The chronology of humanism continued with an eighteenth-century, primarily French movement known as the Enlightenment. Prior to the Enlightenment, the study of people had remained outside the realm of science, treated instead as the domain of theologians. But Enlightenment thinkers, known as **philosophes**, believed the scientific methods refined by Isaac Newton, Galileo, and others could also be applied to the study of human society. Philosophes held members of the Scientific Revolution in high regard; some carried writings of Descartes and Newton with them as if their humanist predecessors were heroes. In all their research, philosophes tried to stay as true and accountable as possible to the scientific method.

Philosophes held widely varying opinions on most social issues, including the role of women, the function of government, and the nature of God. But on one point philosophes agreed: humans are free and individual by nature and to thrive require freedom and reason, not bondage and blind obedience. In fact, if the Enlightenment can be summarized in two words, they would be "freedom" and "reason." Philosophes argued that if individuals were granted equality, freedom, security, and education, people would build better societies, producing more free, reasoning people, who in turn would produce still better societies, and so on. Some philosophes believed that given proper conditions, humans could create a perfect society. This was a major departure from the traditional teaching that humans are fallen, sinful creatures who should not aspire and should obediently accept the station God has appointed, even if it is suffering.

The Enlightenment produced some of the great thinkers of the modern age, Voltaire, Rousseau, and Diderot. Some of the early American revolutionaries were also members of the Enlightenment, or at least the intellectual children of the Enlightenment. Benjamin Franklin is the usual example of an Enlightened founding father, but in fact the American Revolution was itself a political expression of enlightened humanism. The principles described in the Declaration of Independence reflect the Enlightenment in the concept that people are born neither sinner nor saint, king nor peasant, male nor female. What a citizen becomes and how a citizen contributes to society depends on society's protection of the individual's freedom and reason.

The humanist movement moved into the political sphere with the French and American Revolutions. Using Enlightened thought as a foundation and drawing on the traditions of the Renaissance, the Reformation, and the Scientific Revolution, modern revolutionary states, including the United States, established an ideal of inclusion that far surpassed the practices of classical city-states. And while those societies have not achieved the levels of equality and freedom proclaimed in their own revolutionary documents, the original humanist goals persist.

PROJECT 21
Interpreting the Humanism of Luther and Galileo

Many students today maintain that truth is relative to the degree that if people believe something to be true, it is "true for them." Why would neither Luther nor Galileo, both proponents of freedom, endorse such a relativistic principle?

Interpreting the Declaration of the Rights of Man and Citizen

The premier political manifesto of the French Revolution was the **Declaration of the Rights of Man and of the Citizen**. Written in 1789, the declaration still holds the force of law in France today.

Read through the declaration in appendix 8 to answer these questions:

1. In what way is the Declaration of the Rights of Man and of the Citizen "enlightened"?

2. Which passage endorses the Enlightenment principle of "equality"? How is "equality" consistent with the other modern humanist ideals of freedom, reason, and individuality?

3. It is plain to see that people are not equal in the sense that all people have the same abilities, skills, shapes, sizes, backgrounds, and so on. What, then, do the American humanists mean when they claim that "all men are created equal"?

(*continued*)

4. Which passage of the French declaration suggests women should or should not be included in the public process?

5. Are there passages that could endorse discrimination on the basis of skin color? Which key word that appears in these passages might be perverted or used to defend a discriminatory practice?

THE UNITED STATES IN WORLD HISTORY: HUMANISM

Historians look for institutions, traditions, rituals, laws, vocabulary, and so on that perpetuate or promote patterns and establish continuum in culture and society. For example, institutions of education, military, law, and advertising have promoted concepts of nationalism and patriotism in the United States of the twentieth century, but how have religious institutions participated in encouraging or discouraging national or patriotic ideals?

Historians also look for exceptions in history, such as objectors, innovators, revolutions, or changes. What might cause a tradition to endure in one society but to disappear in another? These are often difficult questions and can draw in many factors.

The United States presents some interesting problems in world history. The United States entered the world scene as an independent state founded on the humanist principles of the Enlightenment: freedom, individual citizenship, and equality. Yet the nation was built on economic systems of slavery and the oppression of native people. The United States has fought international wars against oppressive regimes and promoted democracy throughout the twentieth century yet segregated its own population. As a result, the United States stands as a symbol of freedom and progress to some around the world, but to others it appears anti-humanist. Such complexity and paradox is the type of problem historians seek to understand.

PROJECT 23
American Humanism

1. What can you identify (historical or present) in the United States that demonstrates continuity with humanist values? Explain how each item you name endorses humanist thinking.

   Institutions:

   Values:

   Laws:

   People (individuals):

2. What elements seem to break with humanist values? Explain how each item you name breaks with humanist thinking.

   Laws or policies:

   Institutions:

   Popular culture:

   People (individuals):

CHAPTER 6

The Individual and the Institution in History

HUMAN BEINGS descend from a single source, a single location, language, and culture. But as groups left the original African homeland and migrated to new locations, cultural patterns revised, interpreting the same human creature and its environment in new ways. As more groups migrated and groups out-migrated from transient groups, people founded homelands and abandoned homelands and cultures encountered other cultures. People who were separated by generations, centuries, or longer came into contact with reflections of themselves, or **the Other**. *Other* is a term that refers to a person or type from outside the community, an "outsider." A Confucian in a humanist society, for example, could have the perspective and be seen as the Other, and so, too, might a humanist in a Confucian society.

Even where there is the appearance of isolation, people are nevertheless migrating, trading, and exchanging. And when "outside" groups meet one another, they connect to cousins who have developed and acquired new ways of doing things, new words, new technologies, new tendencies of many kinds. This is the story of world history: people connect and exchange when they encounter long-lost cousins. Perhaps many conventional accounts of contact between groups describe primarily war, suffering, prejudice, and judgment. When one culture encounters another, it seems there is most commonly a story of aggression, territorial disputes, friction over religious interpretations, claims to property, inheritance, rule, or law. Such simplified descriptions of human relations are commonly perpetuated by both victor and vanquished, often to serve political interests. Certainly humanity has an impressive record of fear, exclusion, and prejudice. But such a picture is incomplete, even dishonest, without its counterparts, exchange and inclusion. Human connections rarely, if ever, involve a sudden encounter between one dominant and one subordinate society, concluding with the conquering of the one and the disappearance of the other. Encounters are more complex than that.

Most contact between people and cultures is gradual or ongoing; interaction is fluid, as dynamic with peaceful exchange as with violence and prejudice. People marry, borrow, trade, and exchange perpetually with other people, from near and far. Through such activity, human civilizations grow and advance.

In the larger worlds of exploration, war, trade, and other types of large-scale exchanges, a single individual performs roles in his or her life that have impact on society and even on history. In his 1964 Nobel Prize acceptance speech, Dr. Martin Luther King Jr. said, "I refuse to accept the idea that man is mere flotsam and jetsam in the river of life, unable to influence the unfolding events which surround him."[1] Each individual, sometimes through minor acts of compliance, participation, or even silence, might contribute to larger processes of society and of history. This is an important—if somewhat overlooked—theme in history and can be found in most historical examples of cultural contact between contrasting societies or people. One specific example comes from the ancient **Silk Road** and presents an individual's choice of conscience which has implications far beyond the individual.

Around thirteen centuries ago, the monk **Xuanzang** (an older spelling is Hsien-tsang) left China to "find truth" in the west by studying and bringing home Indian Buddhism. His work is a rare example of a person who sets out deliberately and consciously to learn from a foreign culture, in this case to educate his own people about the religion and culture of India. The route he took along the Silk Road was traveled by many different people and cultures, most strange to him. After sixteen years of research and collecting, Xuanzang returned home with stories of the strange lands and people he met along the way. One story he told was of a young soldier, the Turk Khan Yeh-hu.

> The son of the Khan Yeh-hu (or She-hu), belonging to the Turks, [was] rebellious, [and] broke [camp] and marched at the head of the horde, desiring to obtain the jewels and precious things with which it [a nearby convent] was enriched. Having encamped his army in the open ground, not far from the convent, in the night he had a dream. He saw Vaisravana Deva, [a god] who addressed him thus: "What power do you possess that you dare to overthrow this convent?" and then hurling his lance, he transfixed him with it. The Khan, affrighted, awoke, and his heart penetrated with sorrow, he told his dream to his followers, and then, to atone somewhat for his fault, he hastened to

1. Martin Luther King Jr., "Acceptance Speech," in *Les Prix Nobel en 1964*, ed. Göran Liljestrand (Stockholm: Nobel Foundation), accessed December 29, 2015, http://www.nobelprize.org/nobel_prizes/peace/laureates/1964/king-acceptance_en.html.

the convent to ask permission to confess his crime to the priests; but before he received an answer he died.[2]

Xuanzang's story contained a moral for the Turks as well as the Chinese of Xuanzang. Perhaps the moral was that greed and the abuse of power lead to spiritual ruin. In a Confucian tradition, the lesson would have applied not only to commanders such as the son of Khan Yeh-hu but also to heads of state, diplomats and civil servants, teachers, mothers, and individuals at all levels of society and would have had to do with "harmony," "benevolence," and "following one's nature."

A second historical example of conflict between personal inclinations and institutional pressures comes from the history of English-French competition in North America. The story describes a situation similar to that of the son of Khan Yeh-hu in that one individual's personal conscience came into conflict with a larger, institutional mission, and the individual was forced to choose between them. In the middle of the eighteenth century, England seized control of Nova Scotia from France, and King George II demanded the allegiance of the French-speaking settlers in Nova Scotia known as Acadians. In 1755, the king ordered his subordinate, Colonel John Winslow, to issue the order that Acadians either submit or be immediately expelled from their homes and the province. The king's order left the colonel in a moral dilemma because he was well aware of the great suffering his order would create. Winslow understood that executing the order was inhumane and would cause not only the unjust loss of home and property for many innocent, hard-working families but also the loss of life. He issued the order in 1755 and sent thousands of Acadian families to flee Canada for the Caribbean, France, Louisiana (becoming Cajuns), and other far-flung parts of the world. Many died on the road, while others hid in the surrounding forests or went into hiding in neighboring Quebec to seek (though rarely to receive) protection from the French-speaking people of Quebec. Some Acadians were sheltered by local Micmac Indians. Some Acadians returned years later to establish homes again in the Maritime Provinces, particularly in New Brunswick.

But on September 5, 1755, Colonel Winslow issued the order at Grand Pre, Nova Scotia, with this remarkable personal statement:

> Gentlemen, the part of Duty I am now upon is what thoh Necessary is Very Disagreeable to my natural make and Temper as I know it must be Grievous to you who are of the Same Specia. But it is not my Business to annimedvert, but to obey Such orders as I receive and therfore

---

2. Hsien-tsang and Samuel Beal, *Si-Yu-Ki, or, Buddhist Records of the Western World* (London: Trubner and Co., 1884), 45.

without Hessitation Shall Deliver You his Majesty's orders and Instructions vizt.

That your Lands and Tennements, Cattle of all Kinds and Live Stock of all Sortes are Forfitted to the Crown with all other your Effects Saving your money and Household Goods and you your Selves to be removed from his Province.[3]

3. *Report and Collections of the Nova Scotia Historical Society for the Years 1882–1883, Volume III* (Halifax, NS, 1883), 94.

PROJECT 24
The Moral Dilemmas of the Son of Khan Yeh-hu and Colonel John Winslow

1. How do the two stories suggest an individual of apparently minor position in society might still have opportunities to make an impact on the world around him or her that can have historical consequences?

2. How does the story of Khan Ye-hu relate a Confucian ethic?

When people from one culture connect with people from another, there is potential for both institutional and personal friction. When the British solidified colonial rule in India two hundred years ago, they brought with them attitudes of superiority and arrogance that did not allow them to view the Indian culture as being as legitimate a culture as their own. The British, because of a combination of pseudoscientific racial beliefs, economic motivations, and a contempt for any society with a scientific method less modern than their own, did not view Indian people as equal to the British. Institutions that constructed these attitudes spanned the breadth of British society. Educational institutions taught history, geography, and literature from nationalistic and sometimes racist perspectives. Government policies cooperated with corporate and business interests to endorse attitudes that colonies and the native inhabitants were commodities for technological societies to exploit. Churches also endorsed these attitudes by teaching that people who had not entered the modern scientific world were backward, ignorant, and in need of moral conversion to British models and did not deserve the rewards of their own land and labor.

In whatever ways an individual is influenced by institutions, one still carries responsibility for one's own behavior and contributions. One of the finest writers of the British colonial experience in India was **Rudyard Kipling**. Himself a colonial, Kipling grew up in India in an environment that reflected the British colonial mentality. Kipling's attitudes toward the people of India are not difficult to locate in his stories, which, while skillfully and sometimes beautifully written, have fallen out of favor in the late twentieth century largely because of their imperial, arrogant, and racist tone. When in the late nineteenth century he saw the United States pursue colonial enterprises in the Pacific, Kipling wrote to the Americans a poem, a warning, as it were, of the reception the Americans could expect to receive from native people in colonial lands. The poem is titled "The White Man's Burden" and is reprinted in appendix 7. One can hear in the tone of the poem Kipling's attitude toward the natives and his empathy with the colonials. While Kipling was a product of institutional perceptions, as a journalist and author he also perpetuated those perceptions.

Mahatma Gandhi also lived in nineteenth-century colonial India, but unlike Kipling the colonial, Gandhi was a native of a colonized country. Gandhi did not approve of English rule in India, and he did not bow to British arrogance. He believed the English mentality was materialistic and English governance was inherently violent. He denied the moral good in the heavier technology of the Europeans and was not convinced that the society that wields greater power wields moral authority. Gandhi led a successful revolt against British rule by encouraging people of India to not comply with British colonial law. Gandhi taught his followers to never resist evil with evil (violence); rather, he taught them to resist evil by not complying with evil's method, to remain peaceful in the face of violence, and to passively resist in the face of force.

Gandhi was a creative thinker, but he had his influences, one of which was the Russian writer Leo Tolstoy. Tolstoy argued that when a person participates in a society that does evil, the person shares in evil. Tolstoy wrote in 1894 in his book *The Kingdom of God Is within You* that civilization means nothing when compared to the "kingdom of God." Tolstoy believed Jesus commanded his followers to not participate in violence; in other words, to answer evil with good. Gandhi read Tolstoy and did not adopt Tolstoy's Christianity, but he adopted Tolstoy's message of noncompliance. He wrote that Tolstoy's book made "all the books given to me . . . pale into insignificance." Tolstoy and Gandhi represent individuals who, through the conviction of conscience, rejected the institutional practices of their own societies and considered personal conscience the final moral authority.

As Gandhi drew inspiration from Tolstoy, Tolstoy drew from Jesus. Tolstoy's entire premise for his work on the kingdom of God was his interpretation of Jesus' Sermon on the Mount. Historians call such links of ideas *intellectual history*. A fourth great statesman and social activist of the intellectual tradition of peaceful change is **Martin Luther King Jr**. King considered Mahatma Gandhi a model and studied Gandhi's writings. King was also a Christian minister and thus brings the idea of responding to war and violence with peace and forgiveness to a complete intellectual circle, from Jesus to Tolstoy to Gandhi to King, the disciple of Jesus.

PROJECT 25
Jesus, Tolstoy, Gandhi, and Martin Luther King Jr.

Read the excerpts from Gandhi (appendix 3), Tolstoy (appendix 10), Jesus (appendix 5), and go to http://nobelprize.org/nobel_prizes/peace/laureates/1964/king-acceptance.html to read Martin Luther King Jr.'s Nobel Prize acceptance speech, and then answer the following questions.

1. Describe in your own words what the four texts the Sermon on the Mount, *The Kingdom of God Is within You*, Gandhi's memoirs, and Martin Luther King Jr.'s Nobel Prize speech share. Support your answer with quotes from each and explain how these quotes represent similar ideas.

2. What are the specific historical complaints of Tolstoy's critics? How does Tolstoy answer them?

3. On what principles did these four reformers challenge prevailing institutional thinking?

As the examples of Gandhi, Kipling, and Winslow demonstrate, where cultures meet there is commonly both opportunity and friction. Sometimes individuals transcend cultural and institutional differences to be constructive rather than destructive in their behavior. Others see differences as threats. One can find in history examples of both types of behavior.

Two accounts of pilgrims climbing Mount Fuji in Japan provide contrasting perceptions of similar historical events. In this case, however, there is not a clear choice between overt violence and courage, as there was with Winslow, Gandhi, and others. Instead, these selections show a more subtle form of choice and prejudice. **Mount Fuji** is one of the great sacred sites of Japan as well as a natural wonder. It has been the subject of Japanese painting, poetry, and pilgrimage for more than a thousand years. Both accounts come from the nineteenth century, one from a scientist conducting research on the mountain, the other from a missionary working in Japan. The scientist is curious about the pilgrims, but his curiosity about the pilgrims' religious activities stands in contrast to the missionary's more opinionated attitude. The documents are *An American Scientist in Early Meiji Japan* (appendix 9) and "Pilgrims on Fu-ji" (appendix 16).

PROJECT 26
Perceptions of Pilgrims on Mount Fuji

1. Do the missionary and the scientist describe similar physical settings and activities? Might one document be used to confirm the historical accuracy of the other?

2. How might these individual encounters be historically significant as encounters between social systems, mentalities, and civilizations?

3. Describe the encounter between the priest and the scientist. Is their exchange respectful? Why does the scientist suppose "liberal minded" is a positive attribute?

The history of relations between Islam and Christianity is replete with familiar accounts of persecution, exclusion, and judgment. Relations between Islamic Iran and European Christianity in the last decade of the twentieth century do not generally betray this image. Yet there is still among European, American, and Iranian societies a great deal of exchange, trade, education, migration, and interaction on many levels. Even where there are negative associations, however, exchange continues. A hostile debate might occur through editorials or on the Internet, for example, and demonstrate bitterness and prejudice, yet both sides might adopt the same technological medium, sharing forms of communication as they adopt innovations from the Other. But more direct appeals for exchange also come from within both societies.

In the twentieth and twenty-first centuries, a professor of history in Iran has called for reform in his country, and in so doing, he has challenged institutional oppression with an argument of conscience. Professor **Hashem Aghajari** of the University of Tehran, an Iranian war veteran, suggested in a lecture he gave in 2002 that the ruling Islamic hierarchy of Iran look to historical European Protestantism for a model on which to build political and religious reform. Professor Aghajari delivered one lecture in particular (see appendix 13) in which he encouraged the Iranian leadership to follow the example of Protestant Christians to challenge tradition and create a more humanistic government and society. For these words Aghajari lost his post at the university, was forbidden to teach for ten years, and was sentenced to whipping and to death by a regional Iranian court. The religious fundamentalists in the Iranian ruling order were unwilling to consider any suggestion they could learn from the European movement; their own truth was complete. Humanism was to the religious leadership a religious insult.

But the leaders of Hashem Aghajari's Iran must deny a great deal to suppose their culture is wholly "original" or neatly segregated from European, Christian, humanist, or other non-Islamic influence. Intellectual traditions cross boundaries even where leaders attempt to stifle exchange. As the great Oklahoma songwriter Woody Guthrie said of another songwriter, "He just stole from me, but I steal from everybody." To this Woody's friend added, "Plagiarism is basic to all culture." The two singers are more intellectually honest than the Iranian religious elite, for *no culture is original* and every practice, every song, every dance, every technology, every individual of the past hundred thousand years has an antecedent. Human culture is a synthesis. Without change and borrowing, human civilization would wither and die.

PROJECT 27
Hashem Aghajari Encourages Reform through Exchange

An edited text of Professor Aghajari's lecture is in appendix 13. After reading the text of his speech, answer the following questions briefly, using quotations and writing legibly.

1. What does Professor Hashem Aghajari mean by "core" and "traditional" religion?

2. Why does he think Islamic humanism should be the stronger?

3. On what basis does he assume a human rights agenda is necessary to humanism?

4. What belief does Aghajari share with Martin Luther?

5. What is the complaint of the people who shout from the audience at the end of his speech?

The Iranian elite's response to Professor Aghajari's appeal was institutionalized segregation and exclusion of cultural differences. The same can be said of the violent British response to Mahatma Gandhi and his followers. In both cases, institutional traditions dictated the outright rejection of the Other.

Toward the end of the Second World War, while the Nazi state was collapsing and the German military retreated west, the Soviet Red Army advanced into territories that are today the Czech Republic and Poland. These regions had been the homes to culturally mixed populations, Czechs, Hungarians, Slovaks, Poles, and others, as well as to several million German-speaking people whose ancestors had lived in the region for centuries. As the Red Army rolled west toward Berlin, Soviet soldiers raped, plundered, killed, and even publicly tortured German residents without regard to any individual German's political past. Atrocities were institutionalized through direct orders from local officers and even on orders from the premier of the Soviet Union, Joseph Stalin. Local Czech and Polish authorities also cooperated with or initiated such persecutions and violence, sometimes for their own material profit. The episode remains one of the great atrocities of the twentieth century. (See appendix 14, excerpted from *Documents on the Expulsion of the Germans from Eastern-Central Europe.*)

Not all who raped or murdered civilians had been themselves the victims of wartime violence and brutality. Many Soviet soldiers who participated in atrocities had been only recently called up to fight and had not personally experienced battle. On the other hand, not all who might have had "cause" for vengeance behaved violently. Documents collected and published in 1952 under the title *Documents of Humanity during the Mass Expulsions* (appendix 15) describe the actions of men and women who, though they had been themselves prisoners of war or were members of a victorious army, and in the face of grave personal danger, made decisions of conscience to resist institutionalized violence. Albert Schweitzer thought so highly of the *Documents of Humanity*, he referred to them specifically in his 1954 speech accepting the Nobel Prize for Peace. Schweitzer said,

> In 1950, there appeared a book entitled *Témoignages d'humanité* [Documents of Humanity], published by some professors from the University of Göttingen who had been brought together by the frightful mass expulsion of the eastern Germans in 1945. The refugees tell in simple words of the help they received in their distress from men belonging to the enemy nations, men who might well have been

moved to hate them. Rarely have I been so gripped by a book as I was by this one. It is a wonderful tonic for anyone who has lost faith in humanity.[4]

Surely this message from the Second World War still carries meaning today.

4. Albert Schweitzer, "Nobel Lecture: The Price of Peace," in *Nobel Lectures Peace 1951–1970*, ed. Frederick W. Haberman (Amsterdam: Elsevier, 1972), accessed August 15, 2005, http://nobelprize.org/nobel_prizes/peace/laureates/1952/schweitzer-lecture.html (15 August 2005).

PROJECT 28
The Personal Conscience as a Historical Factor

1. What is the contrast in behavior described in the set of documents taken from the *Documents of Humanity* (appendix 15) and those taken from *Documents on the Expulsion of the Germans from Eastern-Central Europe* (appendix 14)? (two sentences)

2. Who are the people who performed some of the acts of charity described in the *Documents of Humanity*, and why might this be unexpected? (two sentences)

3. How was violence against women institutionalized in the events described in the two sets of documents? Why did soldiers attack women and girls in particular?

CHAPTER 7

Modernization

WHEN SEVEN centuries ago, Marco Polo returned home from a journey into Asia that lasted twenty-six years, he published his description of the world beyond Venice and the Mediterranean. His stories were so fantastic that his readers, many of whom had never ventured outside the village, town, or region of their birth, did not believe him. Some of his accounts were indeed outrageous, like the descriptions of birds so large they carried elephants. To a modern reader, however, much of what Marco Polo described appears normal, sometimes even mundane. But to many Venetian readers of the thirteenth century, images of the grand courts of China, the life of the Mongols, the high mountains of central Asia, and exotic religious and marriage practices of India and southeast Asia were so exotic that they seemed otherworldly. People—even educated, reading people—contemporary to Marco Polo lived in worlds that had very limited access to cultures and practices of the Other.

The Travels of Marco Polo was one of the most popular books published in medieval Europe. People are often curious about the Other; they learn from other people, compare their own practices and beliefs, empathize, improve, or compete with the Other. Comparison benefits society; it brings self-awareness. Marco Polo concluded his book with the statement, "I believe it was God's pleasure that we should get back in order that people might learn about the things that the world contains. Thanks be to God! Amen! Amen!"[1]

Marco Polo was one of only a handful of people from any European country to travel to China in the entire century in which he lived. By contrast, in the single year 2000, more than twenty-five million passengers flew in or out of Fiumicino Airport in Rome. Almost thirty-three million passengers

---

1. William Marsden and Manuel Komroff, *The Travels of Marco Polo* (New York: Boni and Liveright, 1926), 351.

passed through Hong Kong International Airport, twenty-one million in or out of Beijing Capital, the city of Marco Polo's host, Kubulai Khan. For a few hundred dollars, any Italian can fly to Beijing in less time than it took Marco Polo to get fifty miles outside of Venice. The modern era multiplied enormously the encounters between societies, and modern technology continues to bring people together in unprecedented numbers. People move and travel more frequently, farther and faster, than ever before. The past two hundred years have accelerated the speeds we travel and communicate so much that in some ways, society has changed more in the past two hundred years than in the previous five thousand.

The armies of Napoleon at the start of the nineteenth century traveled and communicated with more or less the speed and efficiency of the armies of ancient Persia and Greece. By century's close, entire armies were transported rapidly across continents by rail while heads of state communicated by telegraph at the speed of electricity. Today armies travel by jet and generals communicate by satellite transmission. As armies travel and communicate at tremendous speeds, so do families, educators, doctors, and immigrants. The world has never been so small, and people have never had the degree of contact and interaction with foreign cultures that they do today. But these modern developments are not universal. The twenty-first-century world has evolved into two enormous camps: those who share modern technological advantages and those who do not. Between those cultures that have the advantages, exchange, connections, and encounters are constantly advancing.

Although great changes in technology and information occurred during the twentieth century, most of the political and industrial basis for the innovations that brought us here have roots in the century of **industrialization** and **nationalism**, the nineteenth century. These two forces greatly affected the way people encounter, connect, and exchange with one another. *Industrialization* refers to a shift away from a dependence on human, animal, and natural (mostly wind and water) power to a dependence on machine power. Many features accompanied industrialization, such as changes in production from individually produced to mass-produced products, the regimentation of time and labor, and so on. *Industrial revolutions* refers to specific periods of rapid industrialization.

Nationalism refers to the organization of societies and states into *national states* commonly based on "ethnic" definitions. National states are a relatively recent phenomenon, beginning in Europe during the era of industrialization and the French Revolution of 1789. From a "world perspective," nationalism might appear to be the dividing of people into "nationalities," but historically the process was the reverse: national identities absorbed and consolidated local and regional identities. Bavarians became Germans, Lombards became Italians, Cherokee became Americans, and Lapps became

Swedes. The formation of national identities expanded rather than shrank most peoples' perspectives. Before the rise of nations, people generally had identified with villages or parishes, kingdoms, cities, or tribes. Nations did not reinforce as much as assimilate those ancient identities. Nationalist movements conquered and consolidated by centralizing state authority, usually around a single, dominant culture. National and state propaganda claimed where there had once been Sicilians, Venetians, and Lombards, there were now Italians; where there had been Bavarians, Prussians, and Cologners, there were now "only Germans."

But not all newly named citizens welcomed the change. The pattern is clear to see in the history of the United States, where thousand-year-old tribal cultures were destroyed or dismantled in the interest of a national organization that had not existed only decades before. This pattern of "nation building" continued through much of the nineteenth and twentieth centuries. At the start of the nineteenth century, there were one or two **nation-states**; by the end of the First World War in the 1920s, much of the world was organized around sovereign nationalized unions. Nationalist struggles remain unresolved today where borders and "national identities" are not always in agreement. National, ethnic, and regional struggles continue in postcolonial Africa, Tibet and China, Canada and Quebec, Palestine and Israel, and other places as well.

As nationalist movements evolved, they grew in popularity and momentum, eventually generating within nineteenth-century empires popular, nationalistic revolts. Patriots of nineteenth-century "nations without states," including Hungarians, Serbs, Greeks, Irish, Romanians, Poles, Bavarians, and other national groups, worked or fought for independence from Austrian, Russian, British, German, and Ottoman empires. Most nationalist groups hoped to establish new states on ethnic principles, with the rights of sovereignty and **self-determination**. Most claims were made on the basis of "historic" homelands, whether in Europe or elsewhere. Hebrew nationalists, known as **Zionists**, sought a national state in Palestine on the claim that Palestine had been historically Jewish.

Industrialism and nationalism brought the nineteenth-century United States and Europe the power and efficiency to conquer and disrupt, if not dominate, the civilizations of the entire world. Motivations for imperialist enterprises came from nationalism and another, somewhat older force, **capitalism**. Capitalism is a profit-centered economy based on private property, with a tendency toward free markets. Most societies in history have not followed these three principles, and no society has practiced a completely free market. But the humanist concept of freedom, extended to corporations and economically to individuals, emerged in the era of industrialism as the driving force behind much of the colonial and imperialist enterprise. National states set out to claim new markets, capitalize on "untapped" resources (including cheap labor), and convert the people of the world to modern, scientific mentalities. Frequently colonial enterprises gained government backing and sometimes worked in alliance with churches; other times, churches and states came into conflict over the moral consequences of unrestricted competitive economic environments.

Many European Christians opposed capitalism as evil. The cooperation of competitive, profit-driven capitalism with industrial wealth and productivity resulted in deplorable living conditions for many industrial workers and their families. Church groups and socialists in particular protested abuses and encouraged governments to pass labor, market, and health reforms to provide balance for what many saw as an inherently greedy system. Church groups, through the press, from the pulpit, and by other political action, insisted that an unrestricted "free market" was part of a greater "modernism" that should be held accountable to higher moral authority. Churches established their own institutions to counter the ill effects of modern life, to protect the poor, women, and children from profit-driven abuses. **The Salvation Army**, the Red Cross, the YMCA and YWCA, and other charities, orphanages, and poor-assistance groups all date to the nineteenth century.

The nineteenth-century world of expanding markets, new contacts between people, and emergence of new nations created tremendous international friction. One national state opposed the other's colonial activities, out of fear of being outdone, with prestige and markets at stake. The British resisted French incursions into Asia, Germans opposed the French in Africa, Portuguese competed with the British Empire in Asia, the United States and Japan competed in the "game" (somewhat later than the others) in the Pacific, Russia and Japan in eastern Asia and Russia, as well as Austria and the Ottoman Empire in southeastern Europe. Industrial, scientific, and commercial competition was also fierce in the final two decades of the eighteen hundreds and the first years of the nineteen hundreds. On several occasions countries went to war or to the brink of war over colonial disputes.

Diplomatic efforts late in the nineteenth century aimed to limit the unchecked growth of adversarial states. International diplomacy, through shifting alliances and treaties, struggled tirelessly to maintain an international "balance of power" between the "great powers" Great Britain, France, Russia, the German Empire, and the Austrian Empire. The list of states competing for Great Power status included only industrialized or industrializing countries and their subsidiary states. Meanwhile, newer and smaller states struggled to get in on the grand diplomacy of dividing up the globe. Small states feared exclusion from the colonial club would spell imminent absorption. In some cases, such fears proved correct.

In part as a result of colonization and the drive to expand markets, the latter nineteenth century was a period of increased globalization. Globalization was not a phenomenon specifically intended to unite the world into a single civilization or to bring people closer together; instead, **globalization** advanced rapidly because of national and economic competition. Heads of industrial states partitioned the globe into spheres of influence: the British in India, the French in North Africa, the Japanese in China, the United States in North America and the Pacific, and so on. "Spheres" were intended to balance power between industrial states and to consolidate power for the same, but one of the consequences was an enormous exchange of cultures and people worldwide.

Nineteenth-century nations also competed for supremacy in technology, science, and exploration. Nations competed in races to the North and South Poles; in laying the first, the fastest, the longest, the most railroads; the first telegraph connections (1844); the first flight; the fastest voyage across this sea or that ocean; the first to seize an "unclaimed" territory; and the first to use a telephone (1878), a plane, and so on. These "races" and more furthered national reputations and influence and at the same time helped bring distant parts of the world closer together. For this reason, industrialization is sometimes referred to as a development that reduced time and space.

Industrialism also increased the world's population as medicine, transportation, and food production improved. At the time of Christ, the population of the world was around two hundred million people. In 1600 it was around five hundred million. By the middle of the nineteenth century this number exceeded one billion, and since that time it has grown sixfold. Industrialization and its attendant developments created a world that can sustain ever-greater populations. Modern science has improved health care and health access for many people; food production and storage also have seen technological advances. Life expectancy is high and infant deaths are low compared with other times and places in history. Indeed, over the past century and a half, industrialism has transformed all aspects of material culture.

But there is another side to this modern story. Medical, industrial, and technological advances are not accessible to all people. Millions in the world starve. Medical technologies are not available equally to citizens of all nations. Life expectancy is not uniform around the world. In many regions of the earth, whole populations suffer life expectancies little or no higher and infant death rates little or no lower than a thousand years ago. And progress has brought dire consequences as well. In the twenty-first century we are accustomed to descriptions of air and water pollution, dying river systems, depletion of animal species, and global warming, as well as other social consequences that have accompanied industrialization, such as regimentation and alienation.

Early in the era of industrialization it was already apparent to many observers that there were two sides to advances in science and industry. The railroad, that backbone industry of the Industrial Revolution, was a boost in many positive respects. Benefits of the railroad were immediately apparent, and the industry grew in a few decades from nothing to one of the largest industries in the world. The first rail lines were laid in the 1820s, and within fifty years there were more than 150,000 miles of track in use worldwide. But the suffering brought on by work and slums in centers of the coal, steel, and rail industries has been well documented. **Charles Dickens**, **Friedrich Engels**, Emile Zola, and other writers have eloquently painted the picture for us. Industrialization reduced time and space, connected people, and facilitated markets, education, and financial opportunities. But industrialization also brought destruction in at least four areas: the environment, the quality of urban life, the loss of traditional communities, and the destructive capabilities of industrialized militaries. The passage by Friedrich Engels included in the appendix succinctly describes three of these four.

The testimonies presented to the British Parliament in 1844 regarding the conditions of women working in coal mines also show graphically the problems associated with child labor and long hours of industrial work for women. The testimony was part of a successful campaign to pressure Parliament to regulate the coal industry, particularly regarding conditions for women and children. These accounts in particular show clearly how industrialization contributed to the loss of traditional communities.

Deplorable working conditions and the destruction of the environment in industrial centers is both an old and a new story. Patterns of abusive labor practices, unsanitary housing, rampant disease, and intense poverty were regular features of industrial life in the nineteenth century. These same conditions continue in today's industrializing world. In south Asia, treacherous working conditions, particularly for children, are not a recent phenomenon and were not created by industrialization; but increasingly, international, competitive markets have aggravated and multiplied abuses. Children are essentially enslaved by small factory owners who work for large European and American corporations similar to the way children were forced to labor in factories and in mines a century ago in Europe. In 1996 the **Human Rights Watch**, an agency of the United Nations, reported,

> The global leather and footwear industry has changed tremendously in the past decade, moving away from industrialized countries and into developing countries, where labor costs and production costs overall are much lower. As a result of this shift, India's leather and footwear industry has grown astronomically in the past few years, producing shoes, sporting goods, and leather apparel for both domestic consumption and export. . . . Abuses of child and bonded labor laws are par-

ticularly likely to occur in the small house-based "factories" to which shoe-component production is farmed out by contractors. By employing small numbers of people, these subcontractors escape coverage of the Factories Act; by claiming their child workers are members of their family, they escape coverage of the Child Labour Act. . . . Thousands of children are making shoes in the slums of Bombay. . . . They work in tiny manufacturing units that employ three to five children each. These children, mainly boys, are as young as six or seven years old. . . . The boys are trafficked to Bombay from their rural villages. . . . They come to Bombay for ten months at a time, working every day of the month except the days of the full moon and the new moon. Their work days begin at 5:00 or 6:00 a.m. and continue until 10:00 or 11:00 p.m. They sleep at the owner's house, often a small dwelling above or behind the "factory." The children receive no wages for these ten months of nearly constant labor. Instead, their parents receive a payment. . . . The children return to their homes during the two-month period of the monsoon. Their contracts are then renewed, the parents paid again, and the children returned to their masters in Bombay. This cycle continues for ten or fifteen years, beginning at the age of seven or so and continuing until marrying age is reached. . . . We saw children tracing heels on wooden two by fours and cutting them out with motorized saws; cutting women's leather uppers out of leather sheets; stamping brand names on the insoles of shoes and sandals; making the straps . . . and transporting finished products to wholesalers. Every process involved in the manufacture of this footwear was done by children.[2]

Today, labor reform in Asian countries proceeds slowly and parallels the government- and church-led reforms of nineteenth-century Europe and the United States. In the meantime, urban conditions in the industrializing world reflect the wretched conditions common in Europe a century and a half past.

Thus, we can say that the globalizing, modern society is organized around three primary principles: industrialism, capitalism, and nationalism. These developments continue the humanist evolution that began with the Renaissance five hundred years ago. Interpretations of the three principles vary from place to place and from time to time, but their advance has proved thus far all but irresistible.

---

2. Human Rights Watch Children's Project, *The Small Hands of Slavery: Bonded Child Labor* (New York: Human Rights Watch, 1996), 90–92.

PROJECT 29
Industrial Conditions

1. Identify specific examples of the negative impact of industrialization as shown in "Industrial Manchester (1844)" (see appendix 17) and the Human Rights Watch report (earlier in this chapter) on the shoe industry in India.

2. How do "Two Women Miners" (see appendix 17) and "Industrial Manchester (1844)" show the destruction of traditional communities?

3. How do the readings on women miners confirm some of the moral complaints against capitalism and the need for regulation of capitalist industry?

PROJECT 30
Technology and Everyday Life

1. How did industrialism reduce time and space? How is this evident in your own life, in contrast to life in previous centuries? Are these positive developments?

2. Artisans, craftspeople, or other individuals manufactured by hand every man-made thing in Napoleon's world two hundred years ago. How does this compare with your life? Identify things in your life hand-manufactured from raw materials by craftsmen or artisans, and contrast this to the numbers of things in your life manufactured by machine or by people on assembly lines.

CHAPTER 8

Globalization

THE THREE triumphant forces of the modern age—nationalism, industrialism, and capitalism—defined people by nation, ethnicity, and class. While most European states developed parallel industrialized and capitalist societies, enormous friction grew between states from competitive national identities and commercial and colonial interests. Thus, as the nineteenth century came to an end, the world grew closer economically and technologically even as the formation of new nation-states fragmented empires and overwhelmed local associations. Friction in colonial and industrial competition was so intense that, by 1910, a major war between industrial powers seemed unavoidable. Patriots of all nations were confident of their own moral mandate to lead the world into a new age, and many believed in a Darwinian "survival of the fittest" of nations. Thus, Germans, English, French, Italians, and others believed war was not only inevitable, it was desirable. War could prove the worth of the fittest and weed out the weak. The intersection of all these factors finally led in 1914 to a nationalist war on a massive scale, the First World War. And that war was followed by a second, deadlier war of nationalism and world domination in 1939.

In the summer of 1914, patriots of many nations marched to war singing songs and dreaming of glory. Rare was the observer who did not believe his own nation would quickly seize victory and win the day through glory and divine right. Before a few months had passed, however, the fantasy of easy victory had turned into a nightmare. The First World War deteriorated into a defensive war of attrition, glory was dashed, and enthusiasm turned to bitterness. On the battlefields of France, Russia, and Germany, warfare bogged down into defensive networks of trenches that stretched for thousands of miles, filled with rotting corpses both human and animal alongside troops armed with superior defensive weapons and inferior offensive weapons. When officers shouted "over the top" for troops to charge across no-man's land, it was usually a call to a human slaughter, with the attack of infantry or cavalry on horseback no match for machine guns, barbed wire, mustard gas, and heavy cannons firing from the opposite side. Single battles took hundreds of thousands of lives with no change in strategic positions. Alistair Horne reports in *The Price of Glory* that more than seven hundred thousand men lost their lives on a fifteen-mile stretch at the Battle of Verdun alone. Even the United States, which only entered combat in the final eighteen months of the war, suffered around 350,000 casualties. Populations of all belligerent nations became disillusioned, then angry.

As war raged on, citizens, soldiers, and eventually military leaders began to realize the new technological warfare allowed little opportunity for glorious victory. The generation nicknamed the "Lost Generation" because the war deprived them of full, meaningful lives later described the grotesque experiences of the defensive "war to end all wars" in pessimistic poetry, novels, and films. Central to much of the war literature was a picture of lost hope and a wanton destruction of life. Social despair spread across the nations, and a kind of collective depression set in after 1918. Probably the most famous literature of the era is the German novel *All Quiet on the Western Front* by the war veteran Erich Maria Remarque, but many literary works followed similar narratives. The poem "He Went for a Soldier" by Ruth Comfort Mitchell contains many of the most common themes of the literature of the First World War.

He Went for a Soldier

He marched away with a blithe young score of him
With the first volunteers,
Clear-eyed and clean and sound to the core of him,
Blushing under the cheers.
They were fine, new flags that swung a-flying there,—
Oh, the pretty girls he glimpsed a-crying there,
Pelting him with pinks and with roses—
Billy, the Soldier Boy!

Not very clear in the kind young heart of him
What the fuss was about,
But the flowers and the flags seemed part of him—
The music drowned his doubt.
It's fine, brave sight they were a-coming there
To the gay, bold tune they kept a-drumming there,
While the boasting fifes shrilled jauntily—
Billy, the Soldier Boy!

Soon he is one with the blinding smoke of it—
Volley and curse and groan:
Then he has done with the knightly joke of it—
It's rending flesh and bone.
There are pain-crazed animals a-shrieking there;
And a warm blood stench that is a-reeking there;
He fights like a rat in a corner—
Billy, the Soldier Boy!

There he lies now, like a ghoulish score of him,
Left on the field for dead:
The ground all round is smeared with the gore of him—
Even the leaves are red.
The thing that was Billy lies a-dying there,
Writhing and a-twisting and a-crying there;
A sickening sun grins down on him—
Billy, the Soldier Boy!

Still not quite clear in the poor, wrung heart of him
What the fuss was about,
See where he lies—or a ghastly part of him—
While life is oozing out:
There are loathsome things he sees a-crawling there;
There are hoarse voiced crows he hears a-calling there,
Eager for the foul feast spread for them—
Billy, the Soldier Boy!

How much longer, O Lord, shall we bear it all?
How many more red years?
Story it and glory it and share it all,
In seas of blood and tears?
They are braggart attitudes we've worn so long;
They are tinsel platitudes we've sworn so long—
We who have turned the Devil's Grindstone,
Borne with the hell called War!

—Ruth Comfort Mitchell[1]

1. Ruth Comfort Mitchell, *The Night Court and Other Verses* (New York: Century, 1916), 21.

PROJECT 31
Accountability in Ruth Comfort Mitchell's Poem

List agents other than Billy from the poem that encourage Billy's march to war. Include people, symbols, institutions, and culture. Then answer the following question in your own words: to what degree are these elements responsible for Billy's march to war? ("None" is not an acceptable answer. Billy did not go to war alone.)

The wars of no century can match the sheer volume of death and destruction of the wars of the twentieth century. The slaughter of troops was unprecedented in both world wars, but the Second World War brought massive killing of civilian populations as well. In contrast to Old Regime kingdoms where people were subjects, modern democracies identify people as citizens. Unlike subjects, citizens participate in the decisions of the nation-state and are commonly thought to be accountable for the behavior of their leaders. A historical example of this is the contrast between 1815 and 1918. At the conclusion of the Napoleonic Wars in 1815, leaders of the victorious monarchies of Europe exacted punishment on France by convicting and punishing Napoleon personally. He was the emperor, after all, and was held responsible for the decisions of his state. But in 1918, Allied victors meeting at Versailles held the German people responsible for the human and material cost of the First World War. Germany was found **collectively responsible** for the actions of the state. And in the Allied press, treaties, and popular imagination, the concept of "German" defined the enemy. This was also true after the Second World War. This collective, national, ethnic guilt was an invention of the age of nation-states.

The First World War was a disaster for participants, families, and heads of state; nations lost millions of young lives, and governments fell. Four empires collapsed as the former subject people of the Russian, Ottoman, German, and Austro-Hungarian empires revolted and emperors fell from power, were murdered, or fled. In place of those multinational empires, national states were established; Hungary, Yugoslavia, Austria, Czechoslovakia, the Ukraine, Romania, Bulgaria, Poland, and many more nation-states formed to represent ethnic populations. "Successor" states emerged from colonial empires as well. After the unforgivable losses suffered on the battlefields of Europe, citizens of colonial powers refused to support adventurism. Great Britain and France lost colonies around the world, and the United States attempted to retreat into diplomatic isolation.

Despite efforts to isolate, however, advances in communication and transportation spurred globalization. In response to the "world" nature of the war, diplomacy also globalized. After 1918, older states worked with new states to create a balanced, inclusive diplomatic system that recognized smaller as well as larger nations. There emerged a movement to institutionalize a forum for global diplomacy that might prevent another world war. Led by Woodrow Wilson of the United States, the victorious powers assembled a **League of Nations** to ensure that member states,

> In order to promote international co-operation and to achieve international peace and security by the acceptance of obligations not to resort to war,

by the prescription of open, just and honourable relations between nations,

by the firm establishment of the understandings of international law as the actual rule of conduct among Governments, and by the maintenance of justice and a scrupulous respect for all treaty obligations in the dealings of organised peoples with one another,

Agree to this Covenant of the League of Nations.[2]

Founders intended that the League of Nations would prevent war, protect human rights, and promote the right to national self-determination. The success of such goals depended on broad membership, one of the elements the league never achieved. While a majority of European states joined before 1920, Germany did not join until 1926 but then quit seven years later; the Soviet Union entered the league for only six years after 1934; Italy and Japan abandoned the league in the 1930s; and the United States never joined, through no fault of the US president, one of the league's most avid supporters. But the League of Nations left a legacy of cooperation, research, human rights, and a diplomatic forum for a globalizing world.

Nation-states established after the First World War followed the previous model: a centralizing majority defined a "national" concept, usually associated with a language or perception of a culture. But it was not always clear which people might be included as citizens of a new state. There were (and still are) groups in every "national" configuration that did not fit national or ethnic images of the countries in which they lived. There were gypsies in Romania, Jews in Austria, Poles and Bavarians in Germany, Alsatians in France, Macedonians in Yugoslavia, Basques in Spain, and the list could continue into the hundreds of "ethnic" people who did not necessarily identify with the national majority or who were not welcome in the new national communities. As in the nineteenth century, national groups strove to assimilate or expel those people (the Other) who did not willingly adhere to the majority national identities. Sometimes assimilation was dealt with peacefully, sometimes violently.

In the 1930s, chancellor of Germany Adolf Hitler, in an effort to homogenize multinational Germany, formed state policies on the basis of racial stereotypes. Laws defining citizenship, property rights, and legal protections were outlined differently for one ethnic group than for another. While precedent for ethnically based state programs had occurred in other countries as part of the nationalizing processes, the Nazis of Germany merged nationalism and racism with industrialism and modern bureaucracy to "resolve" some of the German minority issues. The German media created propaganda that constructed people of one group or another as "uncivilized," "subhuman,"

---

2. Preamble, *Covenant of the League of Nations*, Lillian Goldman Law Library, Yale Law School Avalon Project, accessed February 1, 2006, http://www.yale.edu/lawweb/avalon/leagcov.htm.

or traitors to the nation. These categories were used as excuses to scapegoat, persecute, and eliminate whole populations. Similar state-sponsored behaviors were repeated in many forums—fascist and other—around the world throughout the twentieth century.

The two greatest wars of the twentieth century have been named world wars because, in the industrial and national age, war can rapidly spread to the entire world. The Second World War was fought with Italy, Japan, and an enlarged fascist Germany on one side and the democracies of the United States, Great Britain, and allies fighting alongside the communist (Stalinist) Soviet Union on the other. The industrialized Second World War attained levels of destruction never before seen. Massive "carpet bomb" and firebomb attacks from the sky, rocket attacks, atomic weapons, blitzkrieg tactics, and concentration camps where millions died made killing large numbers of people easier in the Second than in the First World War. And the principle of "nationality" led military and political leaders on all sides to believe that, as citizens of warring states, civilians were responsible for the actions of their countries and were therefore legitimate targets. Hundreds of thousands of women, children, and other civilians of London, Rotterdam, Stalingrad, Hamburg, Dresden, and Hiroshima died for the actions of their countries in ways that in the prenational age would have seemed irrational. Whereas in the First World War militaries suffered huge losses but civilian populations did not, in the Second World War civilian losses far exceeded military losses. This was caused in large part by the changed perceptions of "nations" and citizens.

While countries entered the war on one side or the other as national states, many people fighting in the Second World War thought more of international than national causes and effects. Leaders, troops, and civilians claimed international justifications and not only the protection of their own countries as just causes for war. Participants claimed human rights and democracy as justifications to go to war against dictators, racism, and oppression. Many who sacrificed in the wars of the twentieth century fought increasingly with a mentality that the world shares a common humanity and a common fate. The latter was frighteningly affirmed in 1945 when the United States detonated atomic bombs over two Japanese cities. It was clear from that day forward that the militaries of the world could destroy everyone on earth. Friend **shared fate** with foe and civilian with military.

After the conclusion of the Second World War, the League of Nations revived under the new name the **United Nations**. Note how closely the Preamble to the United Nations resembles the stated aims of the League of Nations.

We the peoples of the United Nations determined to save succeeding generations from the scourge of war, which twice in our lifetime has brought untold sorrow to mankind, and to reaffirm faith in fundamental human rights, in the dignity and worth of the human person, in the equal rights of men and women and of nations large and small, and to establish conditions under which justice and respect for the obligations arising from treaties and other sources of international law can be maintained, and to promote social progress and better standards of life in larger freedom, and for these ends to practice tolerance and live together in peace.[3]

The United Nations has survived for a half century, during which time the institution has averted nearly countless disasters and alleviated suffering in even more. The international institution has provided enormous quantities of food, medicine, clothing, and shelter to the needy people around the world in times of disaster, natural and man-made. The United Nations was also a critical forum for public, international dialogue between Soviet, US, and Allied interests during the Cold War. The United Nations has developed wider goals, however, while it has also grown more controversial. As the most prominent international organization, it has almost naturally fallen into a position of arbiter of globalization even when war and peace were not immediately at stake.

With every passing year, we see the world shrink not only in time and space but also in economic, environmental, and technological terms. Global influences extend into the political sphere such that people living and working in one part of the world suffer consequences or reap benefits from political decisions made in other, distant regions. Purchases of consumer goods in the United States impact the lives of families in India or small businesses in South Africa or large corporations in Korea. The Internet is creating a single worldwide marketplace. Greenhouse gases emitted from industrial sites in China contribute to the warming of the oceans that moderate the climate in London. In short, the world's economy, environment, warfare, and political spheres have never been as singular as they are today. And tomorrow we will be more global still.

A National Intelligence Council (NIC) report of 2005 (see appendix 18) on globalization, named the 2020 Project, opened its executive summary with, "The very magnitude and speed of change resulting from a globalizing world—apart from its precise character—will be a defining feature out to 2020." The NIC project identifies various reasons why globalization will not reverse despite its detractors. It reports that, while the United States will continue to play an important role, the geographic center of globalization is already shifting and by 2020 will reside in Asia.[4]

---

3. Preamble, *Charter of the United Nations*, United Nations website, accessed February 1, 2006, http://www.un.org/aboutun/charter.

4. National Intelligence Council, *Mapping the Global Future: Report of the National Intelligence Council's 2020 Project*, accessed January 29, 2015, http://www.dni.gov/files/documents/Global%20Trends_Mapping%20the%20Global%20Future%202020%20Project.pdf.

In 1889, visitors to the Paris Exposition who climbed the **Eiffel Tower** witnessed something they had never seen before: the world from the sky. The view from nine hundred feet above the ground was shocking, writes Robert Hughes. People looked the same from the top of the tower; kings and princes blended in with peasants and workers, Parisians were indistinguishable from Englishmen. Society, like the earth, appeared flatter. In the century of modernization, the construction of the Eiffel Tower marks a shift in our perspective; the experience represents what Hughes calls "a pivot in human consciousness."

> The conditions of seeing were also starting to change . . . not so much the view of the tower from the ground, it was seeing the ground from the tower. Nobody except a few men in balloons had ever seen this before. . . . It was the Eiffel Tower that gave a mass audience a chance to see what you and I take for granted every time we fly: the earth on which we live seen flat as patterns from above.[5]

A century after the Paris Exposition, the world received photographs of Earth viewed from space, one solitary blue orb in the empty expanse of the universe. What was in 1889 a rare perspective has today become commonplace.

In 2004 Bill Clinton, speaking at the inauguration of the Bob Dole Institute in Kansas, made the case that if we are careful, globalization can proceed constructively, positively, and peacefully. If we do not take care to proceed with respect, globalization might be our demise. Globalization, after all, seems to be advancing without a pause, pushed on by global corporations, trade, and communications. But Clinton stressed that more powerful societies share the planet with the less powerful, and both carry responsibility to pursue peaceful and generous resolutions to the world's problems. As Pico wrote, we "have the power to degenerate into the lower forms . . . or to be reborn into the higher forms." The truth of the twenty-first century is the world will elevate or degenerate together.

---

5. Robert Hughes, "The Mechanical Paradise," in *The Shock of the New* (New York: McGraw-Hill, 1991), 16.

The Challenge of the Twenty-First Century

Read the speech delivered at the Bob Dole Institute by President Bill Clinton (appendix 12) and the excerpt from the NIC 2020 Project (appendix 18), and then answer the following questions in sentences, in your own words, using supporting quotes from the text.

1. Of the three modern forces that define globalization, only nationalism seems to be under challenge in the twenty-first century. Capitalism and industrialism (as the spread of technology) seem to be growing almost unimpeded, particularly in China, India, Brazil, and elsewhere. But supranational organizations and growing international commerce might be calling into question the principle of national states. Bill Clinton, however, provides some interesting points that could support an argument for the continuing relevance of national states in a globalizing, interdependent world. Please discuss this.

2. What does Clinton mean by the phrase "all this new diversity"?

3. How is Clinton's "all this new diversity" in part a consequence of humanist developments?

(*continued*)

4. How does Clinton say the United States needs to "cooperate institution-ally"?

5. Name two historical models the 2020 Project uses to analyze the present and the future.

6. In what way is globalization a consequence of modern humanist thought? (Write your answer on the back of this page.)

CHAPTER 9

Conclusion
The Silk Road

MOST ATTEMPTS to write world history as the history of progress break down under close scrutiny. For example, one might assume that the history of all societies could be unified under the framework of technological progress. While it is true that technology has advanced from the stone tools of Blombos Cave to today's world, the record of progress is uneven. Ancient Egyptian medicine, for example, was more scientifically advanced than most medicine practiced two thousand years later. Greeks of the classical era also held a higher standard of scientific method than did later societies, as did Mayan, Chinese, and others. And where science succeeds on one front, it fails on the other. What appears to be a technological success today might become an environmental or health disaster tomorrow. Others might say what unifies the history of humanity is the advance of freedom and democracy. But who could maintain that twentieth-century Iroquois live individually more democratic lives than pre-Columbian Iroquois or that Sioux people living on twentieth-century reservations are more free than those of the nineteenth-century plains? Or that Germans of the feudal age were freer than their tribal predecessors? Furthermore, concepts of democracy were more highly developed in classical Greece than in the later Ottoman Empire, yet the Ottomans respected religious diversity more than many of their later successor states. But if "progress" does not describe where we are headed, perhaps there is a different way to approach the question.

Every people and culture on earth arrived where it is today as the result of migrations. People have always been mobile, and this is one activity that has sustained humanity since its beginning. Even during times when people appear to have been sedentary, there were migrations and movements of people. Wars, famines, plagues, pilgrimages, crusades, adventure, study, construction projects, slavery, and any number of personal, family, or national events cause people to wander. Some migrations are well known—the Jews in the desert, for example; several African diaspora; the migrations of Vikings, Huns, Goths, or Magyars.

One of the great migration systems of all time is not named for a particular people but rather for the network of roads and towns that defined it. For two millennia leading to the modern era, the Silk Road connected eastern Asia to central Asia and western Europe. This network of trade routes carried merchants, pilgrims, philosophers, generals, and travelers of all kinds from one empire and people to another, from the courts of China to the ports of Vietnam, from the temples of India to the markets of Samarkand and the streets of imperial Rome. The Silk Road connected hundreds of societies from three continents and was the conduit for the spread of great religions, economies, technologies, empires, and people. So extensive, enduring, and cosmopolitan was the Silk Road network that every person alive today can confidently claim to have had ancestors who lived, traveled, or visited the route.

Like the Silk Road, human civilization and history are fluid and dynamic. We do not see clearly where the human procession is going because it is not headed in a single direction. We are moving in all directions at once, carrying with us ideas, languages, and stories. The superculture of human civilization behaves like the subculture of the Silk Road: mobile, lively, gregarious, borrowing, laughing, loving, fighting, and stealing. Like connections along the Silk Road, every person we meet has a past related to our own, just as every culture ultimately shares ancestry with every other culture. In many ways, we still live on the Silk Road. The study of history empowers the makers of civilization, you and me, to pause along the way, to watch the caravans and processions, merchants, and pilgrims pass by, to witness where they came from and how they interact, and to consider all the places our civilization is going.

PROJECT 33
You, the Migrants

Two hundred years ago, the author's Hertzel ancestors were south German people who emigrated from Switzerland. In the eighteenth century, some of that family migrated to a Lutheran town in Ukraine, where the family remained for less than a century. To avoid persecutions by the Russian government, they migrated to the United States, where they met immigrants from Ireland, and individuals from the two families married. One of their children married into a family descended from Norwegians and Austrians, and that family moved from Missouri to Illinois and then Minnesota. The author then moved to Seattle to work and study, to Oregon to study, and eventually to Oklahoma to teach. The author is also the descendant of Indo-European and Germanic people as well as those who migrated from Africa thousands of years ago.

Almost any person could describe similar events from the past. Some better-known American migrations include Native American "removals," forced and voluntary migrations across the Atlantic from Africa, nineteenth- and early twentieth-century migrations from Europe and Asia, and more recent migrations from Mexico into Texas and the southwest, from Southeast Asia to the Midwest, between Pacific Islands, and so on. Furthermore, each one of us has ancestors who migrated out of Africa across Asia or who participated in other migrations. Such a complicated genealogy of migrations is not unique to the people of North America; we have all been migrating around the world for as long as humans have been human.

In one paragraph, outline your own migrant heritage. What migrations brought you here?

Appendix of Primary Sources

Some readings are prefaced by author introductions, which are set in italics.

1. SOCRATES: A SOCRATIC DIALOGUE BETWEEN MENO AND SOCRATES, RECORDED BY PLATO, 380 BCE

From "Meno," in *The Dialogues of Plato*, vol. 1, trans. Benjamin Jowett (Oxford: Clarendon Press, 1871), 273–74.

Socrates was a philosopher of classical Athens and the teacher of Plato, who recorded Socrates's teaching. Socrates taught that every individual, if properly instructed, carries a capacity to comprehend truth. One method of arriving at truth is to question a person about his or her own beliefs and logic. This is called the Socratic method and is a form of cross-questioning. In this dialogue between Meno and Socrates, the Master begins by asking Meno whether people behave badly because they desire bad things. When Meno responds in the affirmative, Socrates proceeds to demonstrate that the student likely does not believe his own answer. Socrates does not tell Meno what to believe, nor does he tell Meno right and wrong; rather, he guides Meno to the conclusion that in the end Meno reasons for himself. This is the Socratic method and demonstrates a second Socratic principle as well, that each person has an individual conscience and should not accept any belief simply because tradition dictates.

SOCRATES: And does he who desires the honorable also desire the good?

MENO: Certainly.

SOC. Then are there some who desire the evil and others who desire the good? Do not all men, my dear sir, desire good?

MEN. I think not.

SOC. There are some who desire evil?

MEN. Yes.

SOC. Do you mean that they think the evils which they desire, to be good; or do they know that they are evil and yet desire them?

MEN. Both, I think.

SOC. And do you really imagine, Meno, that a man knows evils to be evils and desires them notwithstanding?

MEN. Certainly I do.

SOC. And desire is of possession?

MEN. Yes, of possession.

SOC. And does he think that the evils will do good to him who possesses them, or does he know that they will do him harm?

MEN. There are some who think that the evils will do them good, and others who know that they will do them harm.

SOC. And, in your opinion, do those who think that they will do them good know that they are evils?

MEN. Certainly not.

SOC. Is it not obvious that those who are ignorant of their nature do not desire them; but they desire what they suppose to be goods although they are really evils; and if they are mistaken and suppose the evils to be goods they really desire goods?

MEN. Yes, in that case.

SOC. Well, and do those who, as you say, desire evils, and think that evils are hurtful to the possessor of them, know that they will be hurt by them?

MEN. They must know it.

SOC. And must they not suppose that those who are hurt are miserable in proportion to the hurt which is inflicted upon them?

MEN. How can it be otherwise?

SOC. But are not the miserable ill-fated?

MEN. Yes, indeed.

SOC. And does any one desire to be miserable and ill-fated?

MEN. I should say not, Socrates.

SOC. But if there is no one who desires to be miserable, there is not one, Meno, who desires evil; for what is misery but the desire and possession of evil?

MEN. That appears to be truth, Socrates, and I admit that nobody desires evil.

2. AN ANGLO-SAXON BLESSING FOR THE FIELDS (LATE ANCIENT EUROPE)

From Francis B. Gummere, *Germanic Origins: A Study in Primitive Culture* (New York: Scribner's, 1892), 406–8.

European cultures have long expressed sanctity for the land, the earth, and the regional or local natural settings people occupy. Pagan Europeans in ancient times customarily adopted natural sites, a sacred tree, a spring, or a stone for a site of worship. Fertility, motherhood, and life are powers the land holds in ancient belief. Notions of the sacred power of the land intersect with Christian practice to produce pagan-Christian worship of the earth in rural, popular cultures in central Europe. Some of the concepts described in the following ritual are very ancient, and some still survive today. In the Anglo-Saxon charm, the earth is deemed sacred as the giver of life. One can hardly identify the charm solely as Christian or pagan, so mixed is the language of old and new belief. Holy Mother Earth transcends religious differences, pagan and Christian. Anglo-Saxon priests performed the charm as a remedy for barren fields or for land that had been "bewitched." To a modern observer, this might sound like witchcraft, but it is in fact a prescientific way of understanding nature. God and humanity are united through labor as the earth produces life. Elements of nature symbolically cooperate in the ritual as they are all brought symbolically together. The charm requires participation by all plants, all grains, and so on, since all these elements together signify the singularity of God's universe, and no distinction is made between spiritual and physical things.

Take thou by night, before daybreak, four pieces of turf on the four sides of the land, and note how they previously stood. Take then oil and honey and barm and milk of all cattle that may be on the land, and part of every kind of tree that may grow on the land except hard trees, and part of every known herb except burdock alone, and put holy water thereon and drop thrice on the pieces of turf, and say then these words. . . . And then take the turves to the church, and let the mass-priest sing four masses over the turves and let the green part be turned towards the altar. . . . Then drive the plow and make the first furrow. Say then—

> Hail to thee, Earth, all men's mother,
> be thou growing in God's protection,
> filled with food for feeding of men!

Take then meal of every kind and bake a loaf, "as big as will lie within his two hands," and knead it with milk and with holy-water, and lay it under the first furrow. Say then—

> Full field of food for folk of men,
> brightly blooming, blessed be thou,
> in the name of the holy one, heaven's maker,
> and earth's also, whereon we live,
> God, world-maker, grant growing gifts,
> that all our corn may come to our use!

3. MAHATMA GANDHI (1869–1948)

From Mahatma Gandhi, *The Essential Gandhi: An Anthology of His Writings on His Life, Work, and Ideas*, ed. Louis Fischer (New York: Random House, 1962).

Mahatma Gandhi was an activist who struggled against abuse, prejudice, and colonialism. He worked on behalf of Indians living in South Africa, effecting legal progress toward the protection of human and personal rights. Later, his most famous success came in mass movements he organized against British rule in India. The nonviolent basis for his civil disobedience has made Gandhi a model for human rights activity around the world. Martin Luther King Jr., when he accepted the Nobel Prize for Peace in 1964, said of Gandhi's movement, "Civilization and violence are antithetical concepts. Negroes of the United States, following the people of India, have demonstrated that nonviolence is not sterile passivity, but a positive moral force which makes for social transformation."

[p. 118] I have met practically no one who believes that India can ever become free without resort to violence. I believe repression will be unavailing. At the same time, I feel that the British Rulers will not give liberally, and in time, the British people appear to be obsessed by the demon of commercial selfishness. The fault is not of men, but of the system. . . . The true remedy lies, in my humble opinion, in England's discarding modern civilization, which is ensouled by this spirit of selfishness and materialism, which is purposeless, vain, and . . . a negation of the spirit of Christianity. But this is a large order. The railway, machineries and the corresponding increase of indulgent habits are the true badges of slavery of the Indian people, as they are of Europeans. I therefore have no quarrel with the rulers. I have every quarrel with their methods. . . . To me, the rise of cities like Calcutta and Bombay is a matter of sorrow rather than congratulations. India has lost in having broken up a part of her village system. Holding these views, I share the national spirit, but I totally dissent from the methods, whether of the extremists or of the moderates, for either party relies on violence ultimately. Violent method must mean acceptance of modern civilization, and therefore of the same ruinous composition we notice here. . . .

[p. 157] But I believe non-violence is infinitely superior to violence, forgiveness is more manly than punishment. . . . I want to use India's and my strength for a better purpose. . . . Strength does not come from physical capacity. It comes from an indomitable will. . . .

[p. 166] . . . Civil Disobedience . . . becomes a sacred duty when the state has become lawless or, which is the same thing, corrupt. And a citizen who barters with such a state shares its corruption or lawlessness. . . . It is not so much British guns that are responsible for our subjection as our voluntary cooperation. . . . Our present Non-cooperation refers not so much to the paralysis of a wicked government as to our being proof against wickedness. It aims therefore not at destruction but at construction.

4. OKLAHOMA ALLOPATHIC MEDICAL AND SURGICAL LICENSURE AND SUPERVISION ACT (ENACTED AND REVISED 1994–2013)

From Oklahoma Board of Medical Licensure and Supervision, "Laws for Medical Board," Title 59 O.S., Sections 480–518, accessed June 9, 2004, http://www.okmedicalboard.org.

480. It is the intent that this act shall apply only to allopathic and surgical practices and to exclude any other healing practices. Allopathy is a method of treatment practiced by recipients of the degree of Doctor of Medicine, but specifically excluding homeopathy. The terms medicine, physician and drug(s) used herein are limited to allopathic practice. . . .

492.1. Application forms—Requirements for practicing medicine—Agent or representative of applicant

A. The Board shall create such application forms as are necessary for the licensure of applicants to practice medicine and surgery in this state. . . .

493.1. Contents of application—Requirements for licensure

A. An applicant to practice medicine and surgery in this state shall provide to the State Board of Medical Licensure and Supervision and attest to the following information and documentation in a manner required by the Board:

1. The applicant's full name and all aliases or other names ever used, current address, social security number and date and place of birth;
2. A signed and notarized photograph of the applicant, taken within the previous twelve (12) months;
3. Originals of all documents and credentials required by the Board, or notarized photocopies or other verification acceptable to the Board of such documents and credentials;
4. A list of all jurisdictions, United States or foreign, in which the applicant is licensed. . . .
5. A list of all jurisdictions, United States or foreign, in which the applicant has been denied licensure or authorization to practice medicine. . . .
6. A list of all sanctions, judgments, awards, settlements [etc.]. . . .
7. A detailed educational history, including places, institutions, dates, and program descriptions, of all his or her education, including all college, preprofessional, professional and professional graduate education;
8. A detailed chronological life history from age eighteen (18) years to the present. . . .
9. Any other information or documentation specifically requested by the Board that is related to the applicant's ability to practice medicine and surgery.

   B. The applicant shall possess a valid degree of Doctor of Medicine from a medical college or school located in the United States, its territories or possessions, or

Canada that was approved by the Board or by a private nonprofit accrediting body approved by the Board at the time the degree was conferred. The application shall be considered by the Board based upon the product and process of the medical education and training.

C. The applicant shall have satisfactorily completed twelve (12) months of progressive postgraduate medical training approved by the Board or by a private nonprofit accrediting body approved by the Board in an institution in the United States, its territories or possessions, or in programs in Canada, England, Scotland or Ireland approved by the Board or by a private nonprofit accrediting body approved by the Board.

D. The applicant shall submit a history from the Administration of the Medical School from which the applicant graduated of any suspension, probation, or disciplinary action taken against the applicant while a student at that institution.

E. The applicant shall have passed medical licensing examination(s) satisfactory to the Board.

F. The applicant shall have demonstrated a familiarity with all appropriate statutes and rules and regulations of this state and the federal government relating to the practice of medicine and surgery.

G. The applicant shall be physically, mentally, professionally, and morally capable of practicing medicine and surgery in a manner reasonably acceptable to the Board and in accordance with federal law and shall be required to submit to a physical, mental, or professional competency examination or a drug dependency evaluation if deemed necessary by the Board.

H. The applicant shall not have committed or been found guilty by a competent authority, United States or foreign, of any conduct that would constitute grounds for disciplinary action under this act or rules of the Board. The Board may modify this restriction for cause.

I. Upon request by the Board, the applicant shall make a personal appearance before the Board or a representative thereof for interview, examination, or review of credentials. At the discretion of the Board, the applicant shall be required to present his or her original medical education credentials for inspection during the personal appearance.

J. The applicant shall be held responsible for verifying to the satisfaction of the Board the identity of the applicant and the validity of all credentials required for his or her medical licensure. The Board may review and verify medical credentials and screen applicant records through recognized national physician information services.

K. The applicant shall have paid all fees and completed and attested to the accuracy of all application and information forms required by the Board.

L. Grounds for the denial of a license shall include:

1. Use of false or fraudulent information by an applicant [etc.].

5. THE SERMON ON THE MOUNT (CIRCA 28 CE)

From Matthew 5:21–46 (RSV).

Matthew 5

[21] "You have heard that it was said to the men of old, 'You shall not kill; and who-ever kills shall be liable to judgment.' [22] But I say to you that every one who is angry with his brother shall be liable to judgment; whoever insults his brother shall be liable to the council, and whoever says, 'You fool!' shall be liable to the hell of fire.

[23] So if you are offering your gift at the altar, and there remember that your brother has something against you, [24] leave your gift there before the altar and go; first be reconciled to your brother, and then come and offer your gift.

[25] Make friends quickly with your accuser, while you are going with him to court, lest your accuser hand you over to the judge, and the judge to the guard, and you be put in prison;

[26] truly, I say to you, you will never get out till you have paid the last penny.

[27] You have heard that it was said, 'You shall not commit adultery.'

[28] But I say to you that every one who looks at a woman lustfully has already committed adultery with her in his heart.

[29] If your right eye causes you to sin, pluck it out and throw it away; it is better that you lose one of your members than that your whole body be thrown into hell.

[30] And if your right hand causes you to sin, cut it off and throw it away; it is better that you lose one of your members than that your whole body go into hell.

[31] It was also said, 'Whoever divorces his wife, let him give her a certificate of divorce.'

[32] But I say to you that every one who divorces his wife, except on the ground of unchastity, makes her an adulteress; and whoever marries a divorced woman commits adultery.

[33] Again you have heard that it was said to the men of old, 'You shall not swear falsely, but shall perform to the Lord what you have sworn.' [34] But I say to you, Do not swear at all, either by heaven, for it is the throne of God, [35] or by the earth, for it is his footstool, or by Jerusalem, for it is the city of the great King.

[36] And do not swear by your head, for you cannot make one hair white or black.

[37] Let what you say be simply 'Yes' or 'No'; anything more than this comes from evil.

[38] You have heard that it was said, 'An eye for an eye and a tooth for a tooth.'

[39] But I say to you, Do not resist one who is evil. But if any one strikes you on the right cheek, turn to him the other also; [40] and if any one would sue you and take your coat, let him have your cloak as well; [41] and if any one forces you to go one mile, go with him two miles.

[42] Give to him who begs from you, and do not refuse him who would borrow from you. [43] You have heard that it was said, 'You shall love your neighbor and hate your enemy.'

[44] But I say to you, Love your enemies and pray for those who persecute you, [45] so that you may be sons of your Father who is in heaven; for he makes his sun rise on the evil and on the good, and sends rain on the just and on the unjust.

[46] For if you love those who love you, what reward have you? Do not even the tax collectors do the same?"

6. LIFE AMONG THE ZULU: THREE TEXTS (1870)

From Henry Callaway, *Religious System of the Amazulu, in the Zulu Language with Translations into English* (Springvale, South Africa: John A. Blair, 1870), 185–96, 259–62, 361–74.

The readings describing life among the Zulu are taken from Henry Callaway's nineteenth-century record of life among the African people. The readings are useful as, among other things, examples of animism. Animism is one of humanity's oldest beliefs about the spiritual world, death, and God. In these readings, as in other primary readings, you will understand them in their own context only when you read them with an open mind. Try not to look for justifications or affirmations of your own perspectives, but try instead to read these texts as they were understood by the cultures they describe. Do you see evidence in these texts that suggests life is present in all things (animism)? How are the living related to the dead, not only in a genealogical sense but in a present, dynamic sense?

Amatongo narrates the story of a Zulu convert to Christianity. The word Itongo *is used to describe a spirit of the dead.*

Amatongo

The account of the illness of James, which is not intelligible among Christians; for although a person may appear to be affected with those symptoms which precede the power of divination, yet when he goes to a mission station all that ceases through continually hearing the word of God. There are many who were so affected, but are now so no longer. But as regards him who is now so old, it is marvelous that he should begin to be so affected, as though he had only just come to a Christian village.

I and Paul reached the place where he is, going with the intention of taking him by surprise, saying to each other, "Do not let him hear or see us; let him first see us when we are already in the hut, before he puts himself to rights, that we may see what he does now when no man is looking at him."

When we came he was lying down covered with two blankets—one black, the other grey and old. When he saw us he remained lying and was silent. I aroused him, saying, "Arouse." He writhed himself and said, "Just have patience. I am about to arise. Make haste and tell me! Make haste and tell me! What has happened at home?" But was a long time before he arose. At length he arose and saluted us; and we saluted him. I asked him, saying, "James, how are you?" He said, "I am very ill." I said, "What is the matter with you?" He said, "I have a disease with which I am not acquainted." I said, "Tell me all about it." He began by saying: "O, truly, you are right. If it were a mere boy who asked, I would not say a single word. But since it is you who ask, I will tell you everything. At first I was afraid, and said, 'What will men say?' But now since this disease has separated me from you, I can make no concealment.

"Long ago this disease began, even before I quitted the house on the other side of the river to go to my new house; it began whilst I still lived in the village. And the family of Umapontshi know it. But it passed off again. It first began by creeping up from my fingers and toes; it then crept up my arms and thighs; it ran and spread itself over the whole body, until it reached the upper part of the body, and stopped in my shoulders, and caused a sensation of oppression, and there was a great weight here on my shoulders; it was as if I was carrying a heavy weight.

"But now it is not that only; but now there are things which I see when I lie down. When I left home I had composed three songs, without knowing whence they came; I heard the song, and then just sang it, and sang the whole of it without having ever learnt it.

"But that which troubles me most now is, that there is not a single place in the whole country which I do not know; I go over it all by night in my sleep; there is not a single place the exact situation of which I do not know. I see also elephants and hyenas, and lions, and leopards, and snakes, and full rivers. All these things come near to me to kill me. Not a single day passes without my seeing such things in my sleep.

"Again, I see that I am flying, no longer treading on this earth."

I asked him, "Since it is thus with you, do you still remember your Lord?"

He said, "No. To do so is death to me. If I try, saying, 'Let me pray,' it is as if I summoned all kinds of death to come and kill me at once. The Lord's tidings are plucked out of me by this disease. It alone has now the dominion over me."

I said, "Do you remember that old dream of yours?"

He said, "Do you speak of that of the boats?"

I said, "Yes."

He replied, "Oh! I do not forget it. I see clearly now that the boat is my faith, which has now sunk into the water. And the dogs which I saw are now devouring me."

I said, "But if your Lord is now your enemy, who will save you?" He replied, "No. I am now dead altogether. I do not think that I am still a man who can enter into a new position, which I do not in the least understand. I do not know what I am. Attend, for I am a man who loves my children dearly. But now I do not care whether they are alive or not. The great thing is this disease alone."

He continued, "And now I begin to go out by night, having an internal intimation about medicine; it is said, 'The medicine is in such a place; go and dig it up.' I go out and reach the place, but do not find the medicine; I merely walk up and down, and at length return. This is my present state.

"There are many things which I seem to see, but when I go to them I cannot see them. At length it happened one day very early in the morning, I was told to go and dig up some medicine. I went to the place, but did not see the medicine, and came back again. When I reached home, it was said, 'Why have you left the medicine? It is that which you saw. Go and dig it up.' At length I went to the place and dug it up. Again I threw it away, for I did not know what to do with it. I was told to go and dig up another medicine on the Isithlutankungu. I refused, and I have not been to this day.

"But the great thing is meat; it is said constantly, 'Let a bullock be killed.' It is as though I could eat meat daily. This disease longs for meat; but I will not kill cattle. I am harassed by the dogs; it is as if where I am the dogs must not be beaten; I am greatly afraid of the noise. And it is as though I could not look on a diviner; he may come, I am at once in a dying state, and fall down and die. It is this, then, that troubles me. And now I no longer love any one. My heart no longer loves men. It is as though I could stay where it is perfectly still—where there is not the least sound. When you tell me to return, I do not know where I could stay, for the bell of our village sounds again and again. I do not like such a sound as that; I am much afraid. I shall not stay. I shall be driven away by the bell."

And then we spoke of his return, I saying, "Come home, if you are ill here; your wife, not seeing you, does not suppose at all that you are under medical treatment. To her way of thinking, you have merely forsaken her; therefore when her father comes he will come and take her away with him. You know yourself that our wives talk, and although a man is not sick, they tell us that if a husband rebels and returns to a heathen life, attracted by its pleasant things, yet his wife, because she does not know any pleasant things of heathen life, will at once separate from him, and not die with the death with which another wilfully kills himself. Do you not know that our wives say thus?"

He assented and said, "Yes. Hannah came here some days ago. She told me to get rid of this disease. And if I did not get rid of it, we should separate. I answered her and asked, 'What is meant by getting rid of it? Am I fond of it? Did I produce it? O, I do not know how the disease can be got rid of. The disease is master of the sick man.' And so we separated. And I am now about to return home for that saying of hers, 'If the disease does not cease we shall separate.' I will now come back, that my wife see for herself that which can get rid of the disease. I cannot fix the day. You will see me when I come. My body is in pain, for on the night before you came I saw you coming to me, but you were white men. A white man hurt me; he came in here and struck me on the thigh which was broken and broke it again. I arose and threw ashes over him. I am ill from that then. I cannot tell you the day.

"I am not ill every day. Some days I am quite well, especially on Sunday. On Sunday, although I no longer know it is Sunday, I am very well. I now know by my body that it is Sunday. Such then is my disease.

"Go. I will accompany you; I will come back from the top of the hill."

So then we went with him. But he now goes naked, and wears the umuntsha. I just caught sight of his umuntsha; the hinder part was black.

Further, I asked him, "Why did you leave home unknown to our Teacher, who is a doctor of all diseases, without telling him?"

He replied, "I did not tell him, for I was afraid, and said, 'If I tell him, he will say I am mad, and seize me and send me to Pietermaritzburg, and I shall stay there a long time.' I feared that then, and did not tell him, thinking, 'O, since a mad man destroys people's property, and I do no harm, but my sickness is an injury to myself only;—O, no, let me not tell him. It may be I shall get well if I find doctors for myself. Let me go.' So I went away."

So we left, and separated from him at a place above the village. He walked without limping; his thigh has not dried up, it is of the same length as the other. But when he is going down hill, it is evident that he is a man who has been injured. But when he goes up hill, he looks like all other men.

There are only three kinds of food that he eats—meat, and the dregs of beer mixed with boiled maize; if these cannot be had he eats wild herbs. That is the food on which he lives. He does not put amasi into his mouth by any means; he dislikes it, and it disagrees with him.

Again, once at night he was told to awake and go down to the river, and he would find an antelope caught in a Euphorbia tree; and to go and take it. "So," said he, "I awoke. When I had set out, my brother, Umankamane, followed me." He threw a stone and struck an aloe. James was frightened, and ran back to him and chided him, saying, "Why did you frighten me when I was about to lay hold on my antelope." That was the end of it, and he was not again told by any thing to go and fetch the antelope. They went home, there being nothing there.

James's people say they are of a family who are very sensitive, and become doctors. There are two of his brothers in Zululand who are doctors. James told me, saying, "Heber came to us on his arrival from Zululand; he told me that my brothers in Zululand are now doctors, So-and-so and So-and-so." And so James said, "He then is the man who brought this disease on me. Whilst he was telling me I was seized with a fearful dread. I did not answer him, but remained silent. I am now ill because he spoke of what I myself was experiencing; but I did not speak of it, for I did not know what disease it was. He made me understand; and I understand it to this day." It is said that James's father, Ukokela, was the steward of the Zulu king. But he was seized with the disease which precedes the power to divine. The king was angry when he heard it. He ate up all his cattle. That was the medicine which cured Ukokela. That was the end of it.

Others are doctors here in the country of the English. His sisters have the initiatory symptoms; there are many who have James's disease. Some have the Itongo laid. With others the disease ceases of its own accord; it is tired, and leaves them. Another, not one of James's relatives, I heard Ujojo mention her; she was a girl of the Abambo, the daughter of Unoponya; it is said, she was affected, and did as James does. But she was treated by many doctors. They could not cure her; she still went to the mountains, and did not stay at home; she was a married woman. At length she was treated by Ujojo, the son of Umanzezulu; he cured her. He killed two goats—or, rather, a sheep and a goat; the goat was white, the sheep black. He treated her with them; the black sheep made the Itongo indistinct, and no longer bright; the white goat made the Itongo white and bright, that it might make her see clearly. So he laid the Itongo, and she went home; he caused her to live at home. And she is now a human being. It is said, for a long time she lived in the mountains. But it is now no longer apparent that she ever did so.

The diviners tell James that he too is beginning, and will soon be a doctor. But they say he must not be treated with black medicines to lay the Itongo, for he will die; he must be just left alone. His friends therefore do not know what to do, since it is said, he will die. They merely look on. The diviners' word is their law; they can on no account go beyond it.

Becoming a Doctor

Divining with Sticks and Bones

The account of diviners when they begin to enter on divination. No one knows that a man will be a diviner. He begins by being affected with sickness; it appears about to cease, but it does not. It is in this respect at the commencement that diviners, and those that have familiar spirits, are alike; they differ in their mode of divination, for the diviner with familiar spirits does not resemble another diviner.

When a diviner divines for people, even he tells back to the people the truth which he first took from them. If as regards that which is done by the diviner we put all together, we shall say, it is the people who divine; for the diviner does not begin with any thing that he has not heard from the people who come to divine.

The Initiation of a Diviner

The condition of a man who is about to be an inyanga [note from the translator on the use of the word "Izinyanga".—It is, perhaps, better to retain the native word than to translate it by a word which does not fairly represent it. Inyanga, generally rendered doctor, means a man skilled in any particular matter = magus. Thus, an inyanga yokubula is a doctor or wise man of smiting, that is, with divining rods—a diviner. Inyanga yemiti, a doctor of medicines. Inyanga yensimbi, a smith, &c.] is this: At first he is apparently robust; but in process of time he begins to be delicate, not having any real disease, but being very delicate. He begins to be particular about food, and abstains from some kinds, and requests his friends not to give him that food, because it makes him ill. He habitually avoids certain kinds of food, choosing what he likes, and he does not eat much of that; and he is continually complaining of pains in different parts of his body. And he tells them that he has dreamt that he was being carried away by a river. He dreams of many things, and his body is muddled and he becomes a house of dreams. And he dreams constantly of many things, and on awaking says to his friends, "My body is muddled to-day; I dreamt many men were killing me; I escaped I know not how. And on waking one part of my body felt different from other parts; it was no longer alike all over." At last the man is very ill, and they go to the diviners to enquire. . . . He is possessed by the Itongo. There is nothing else. He is possessed by an Itongo. . . . If you bar the way against the Itongo, you will be killing him. For he will not be an inyanga; neither will he ever be a man again; he will be what he is now. If he is not ill, he will be delicate, and become a fool, and be unable to understand any thing. I tell you you will kill him by using medicines. Just leave him alone, and look to the end to which the disease points. Do you not see that on the day he has not taken medicine, he just takes a mouthful of food? Do not give him any more medicines. He will not die of the sickness, for he will have what is good given to him.

So the man may be ill two years without getting better; perhaps even longer than that. He may leave the house for a few days, and the people begin to think he will get well. But no, he is confined to the house again. This continues until his hair falls off. And his body is dry and scurfy; and he does not like to anoint himself. People wonder at the progress of the disease. But his head begins to give signs of what is about to happen. He shows that he is about to be a diviner by yawning again and again, and by sneezing again and again. And men say, "No! Truly it seems as though this man was about to be possessed by a spirit." This is also apparent from his being very fond of snuff; not allowing any long time to pass without taking some. And people begin to see that he has had what is good given to him.

After that he is ill; he has slight convulsions, and has water poured on him, and they cease for a time. He habitually sheds tears, at first slight, and at last he weeps aloud, and in the middle of the night, when the people are asleep, he is heard making a noise, and wakes the people by singing; he has composed a song, and men and women awake and go to sing in concert with him.

Therefore whilst he is undergoing this initiation the people of the village are troubled by want of sleep; for a man who is beginning to be an inyanga causes great trouble, for he does not sleep, but works constantly with his brain; his sleep is merely by snatches, and he wakes up singing many songs; and people who are near quit their villages by night when they hear him singing aloud, and go to sing in concert. Perhaps he sings till the morning, no one having slept. The people of the village smite their hands in concert till they are sore. And then he leaps about the house like a frog; and the house becomes too small for him, and he goes out, leaping and singing, and shaking like a reed in the water, and dripping with perspiration.

As to the familiar spirits, it is not one only that speaks; they are very many; and their voices are not alike; one has his voice, and another his; and the voice of the man into whom they enter is different from theirs. He too enquires of them as other people do; and he too seeks divination of them. If they do not speak, he does not know what they will say; he cannot tell those who come for divination what they will be told. No. It is his place to take what those who come to enquire bring, and nothing more. And the man and the familiar spirits ask questions of each other and converse.

The Healing Spirits of the Zulu

I once went to a person with a familiar spirit to enquire respecting a boy of ours who had convulsions. My father and brother and mothers and I wondered what was the nature of the disease, since it was a new thing. We saw at first sight that it was something about which we must enquire of the diviner. We set out and went to the person with a familiar spirit. We made obeisance, saying, "Eh, friend; we come to you for good news." We waited. The doctor said, "Good day." We replied, saying, "Yes." She poured out some snuff, and took it; she then yawned and stretched, and also shuddered, and said, "They who divine are not yet here."

We remained a long time, and at length we too took some snuff; when we were no longer thinking of the reason of our coming, we heard that the spirits were come; they saluted us, saying, "Good day." We looked about the house to see where the voice came from.

The spirits said, "Why are you looking about, for we merely salute you?"

We said, "We look about because we cannot see where you are."

They said, "Here we are. You cannot see us. You will be helped by what we say only."

The voice was like that of a very little child; it cannot speak aloud, for it speaks above, among the wattles of the hut.

We replied to the salutation.

The spirits said, "You have come to enquire about something."

The person whose familiars they were said, "Strike the ground for them; see, they say you came to enquire about something."

So we struck the ground.

They said, "That about which you have come is a great matter; the omen has appeared in a man."

We struck the ground, and asked, saying, "How big is the man in whom the omen has appeared?"

They replied, "It is a young person."

We struck the ground vehemently there, when we perceived that she had hit the mark.

They said, "I say the omen is a disease."

We smote the ground vehemently.

They said, "It is disease in the body of that young person." They said, "Let me see what that person is? It is a boy."

We assented strongly.

They said, "He does not yet herd. He is still small."

We smote violently on the ground.

They said, "But you wonder at what has occurred to him." They said, "Strike the ground, that I may see what that is which has occurred to the body of the little boy."

We struck the ground vehemently, and said, "We will hear from you, for you have seen that it is a little boy."

They said, "There he is; I see him; it is as though he had convulsions."

Upon that we smote the ground vehemently.

They said, "What kind of convulsions are they? Enquire of me." We said, "We have nothing to ask about. For behold you know; you have already first told us. For it is proper that you should tell us to ask, if you were not going the right way; but as we perceive that you are going the right way, what have we to ask of you?"

They replied, "I tell you to ask, for perhaps I am going wrong."

We said, "No; you are not going wrong; you are going by the way which we ourselves see."

They said, "The disease began in the child when he began to walk. When he was very young, you did not see the disease—when he was a little infant; at length when he began to laugh, the disease had not yet appeared; at length he began to sit up, it not having yet appeared; at length he began to go on all fours, it not having yet appeared; at length he began to stand before he was affected by it; when he began to lift his foot from the ground to toddle, the disease came upon him. When you saw the disease, you saw it without expecting anything of the kind; he died in his mother's arms; his mother poured water on him when he was turning up his eyes; she uttered a great cry, you started, and ran into the house; when you entered he had again come to life. The mother said, 'You heard me cry; my child was dead. Do you not see he is wet? I poured water over him for some time, and therefore he has come to life again.'" The spirits continued, "I have now told you this; deny if what I say is not true."

We replied, "We can in no way dispute what you say; we have told you already that you were going by the right path."

The spirits said, "This disease resembles convulsions. You have come to me to know what is this disease which is like convulsions."

We said, "Just so, you say truly; we wish to hear from you, spirit; you will tell us the disease and its nature, that we may at length understand of what nature it is; for you have already told us the name of the disease; tell us also the medicines with which we shall treat it."

They replied, "I will tell you the disease. You are greatly alarmed because you say the child has convulsions; and a child with convulsions is not safe; he burns himself in the fire. I shall tell you what caused this disease. Just smite on the ground, boys, that I may understand if the child is the only son of his father."

We said, "Yes; he is his only son."

They said, "Smite the ground, that I may understand what relation you are to the child, since you come here to enquire."

We smote vehemently on the ground.

They said, "The boy is your brother. Smite the ground, that I may see if he is really your brother born of your own father, or not. Not so. He is not really the son of your father. Your fathers are brothers. He is your brother, because your fathers were brothers."

We smote the ground violently.

They said, "Smite, that I may understand which is the older of the two fathers. I say, boys, your own father is dead. Smite, that I may understand where he died. There he is; I see him; he died, boys, in the open country. He was stabbed with an assagai. By what tribe was he stabbed?"

We smote the ground vehemently.

They said, "He was stabbed by the Amazulu on this side the Utukela; that is where your father died, boys. The father of that child is your uncle, because he was your father's brother; he was the elder of the two."

They said, "Let me now tell you the disease which has attacked the boy. His disease is like convulsions; but it is not convulsions. And you are greatly alarmed because you think it is convulsions. But I shall tell you, for you will not again see him have a fit. I shall tell you what to do when you get home. Did you ever sacrifice for him? You have never sacrificed for him."

They said, "Let me just see where you live. You live among the Amathlongwa; that is the tribe where you live. Let me just see where you were born. You belong to the Amadunga. Just let me see, since you are here among the Amathlongwa, why you were separated from the Amadunga to come here. You quarrelled with your own people, and so came here to the Amathlongwa. Smite the ground, that I may see if you have built your own village."

We smote the ground.

They said, "You have not yet built it. You live in the village of another; you have not yet built your own village on the hill. As for the boy, the disease attacked him in the village where you now are. Smite the ground, that I may see what relation the man with whom you live is to you."

We smote the ground.

They said, "He is your cousin on the mother's side. I see nothing wrong in the village of your cousin; he is good; I see no practicing of sorcery there; I see that the village is clear; you eat with your eyes shut, for you have nothing to complain of. What I shall tell you is this, it is the ancestral spirits that are doing this. It is not convulsions the child has. For my part I say he is affected by the ancestral spirits."

We wondered that we should continually hear the spirits which we could not see, speaking in the wattles, and telling us many things without our seeing them.

The spirits said, "I point out your ancestral spirits. When you reach home you shall take a goat. There it is, a he goat; I see it.

We said, "How do you see it?"

They said, "Be silent, I will tell you, and satisfy you as to its colour. It is white. That is it which has just come from the other side of the Ilovo from the Amanzimtoti. It is now a large he goat. You shall sacrifice it, and pour its gall on the boy. You will go and pluck for him Itongo-medicine. I see that Itongo; it says that your village is to be removed from its present place, and built on the hill. Does not the Itongo ask, 'Why has the village staid so long in the midst of another?' It injures the lad, saying, 'Let the village remove from this place.' The he goat you will sacrifice to your grandmother; it is she who refuses to allow the child to die, for your grandfather had been earnest to kill him, that he might die and be buried in accordance with his wish. I tell you this to satisfy you. I tell you that if the disease returns, you may come back to me and take your money. I tell you that this disease is caused by the ancestral spirit, because it wishes that your village should remove."

The spirits said, "Now I have divined for you; so give me my money."

We took out the money.

Then they said to her whose familiars they were, "Take it; there is the money."

They added, "I just take this money of yours. You will come and take it again if the disease returns. I say, it will never return again."

The woman with the familiar spirits sat in the midst of the house, at the time of full daylight, when we enquired of her; for the spirits cannot go alone when they are going to divine; their possessor goes with them. For if they wish to go they tell their possessor, saying to her, "Let us go to such a place," wherever they wish to go. The possessor of them cannot speak; she usually says little, for she too enquires of the spirits, and says, "So-and-so, when you say so, do you tell the people who come to enquire of you, the truth?" In reply they say, they do tell the truth, and those who come to enquire will see it. She says, "Tell them the truth. They will come to me here if they come to take back their money; and if you tell them falsehoods, I shall give them back their money again. If you do not tell them the truth, I shall give it back to them." The spirits assent, saying, "You may give it back. For our parts we speak truly; we tell no lies."

So the possessor of the spirits took the money.

The spirits said to us, "Go in peace." We wondered, "When they bid us go in peace, without our seeing them. They told us to give their services to all our people at home. We said we would."

They said, "When you get home, do exactly what I have told you." We replied, "Yes; we will do all you have told us to do."

So we went home. On our arrival we found the child better. As we were speaking with him, our father came into the house, and we said, "O father, we never had such confidence in a doctor. When we heard we said, 'The spirit has divined.' The spirits divined; they told us all things—our birth, and the order of our birth, and that he with whom we live is our cousin; they told us every thing. They said the boy has nothing the matter with him that will kill him. They said we are alarmed, thinking he has convulsions; and we assented, saying, 'Yes, yes; we think he has convulsions.' The diviner denied, saying, 'No; he has not convulsions; he is possessed by a spirit. The spirit says that your village must be moved.' The spirits pointed out a white goat, and directed that it should be sacrificed for the child, and the village be moved; and they ordered us to pluck for him Itongo-medicine, and sacrifice the goat. They said, if the disease returned, we were to go and take back our money."

Our father said, "O, they have divined, both as regards the disease and our relations with our cousin. We see they have divined. Why did not our ancestral spirits tell me in a dream that there was something which they wanted, instead of revealing themselves by coming to kill the child in this way? What prevented them from telling me in a dream what they complained about, instead of revealing themselves by coming to kill the child in this way, without saying any thing to me first? These dead men are fools! Why have they revealed themselves by killing the child in this way, without telling me? Go and fetch the goat, boys."

We went to fetch the goat from the house. We killed it, and poured the gall over the boy. Our cousin went to pluck the Itongo-medicine; he squeezed the juice into a cup, and gave it to the boy to drink, and left the cup outside the kraal. The goat was eaten.

We worshipped the ancestral spirits, saying, "We shall see that the child is possessed by a spirit by his getting well, and not getting ill again; we shall say the spirit has lied if he is still ill. We shall see by his recovery; and shall then say, the spirits have told the truth. We do not understand why you have killed such a child as this. What prevents you from making old people ill? That is a good spirit which appears in dreams, and tells what it wants." Such were the words with which we addressed the spirits.

Our father said, "I shall now quit this place with my village in the morning, and put it in a place by itself. Why, when I thought I was living in peace, am I still obliged to be a wanderer? There is a site of an old village; I will examine it well. I shall now remove the village; may the new place be healthy and good, and this boy of mine be no longer ill. If he is still ill, I shall say he is not possessed with a spirit; and I will quarrel with the spirits, and say they have not divined properly." Our father said thus. He said, "I will look at the new site in the morning; let us go together, my cousin, and look at the new site, and inspect it well, for I say I am still a wanderer; for the ancestral spirits have killed me for staying here."

So he and his cousin went in the morning to inspect the site. They went to a place on the river Umathlongwa, and thoroughly inspected it and thought it good, and that it was a proper place for us to build on, for there was water near. They returned home.

In the morning we took our axes, and went to cut wattles and poles for the village. When we had finished cutting, the people of our village left that of our cousin and went to it, and then we completed it. The boy was not ill any more. It turned out in accordance with the word of the spirit; he was not ill again. At length he took out the calves at milking time, and herded the calves; at length he not only herded the calves and goats, but all the cattle—calves, goats, sheep, and cows. And at length he grew to be a man. His name is Umpini. He is now a diligent man. Next year he will milk the cows.

The name of the woman with the familiar spirits is Umkaukazi. It was not a man, but a woman. She saw us for the first time when we saluted her on our arrival; for we too had been told by others that she was a great diviner. She lived on the Umtwalume by the sea, at a distance from us. It is a day and a half's journey from this.

7. RUDYARD KIPLING, "THE WHITE MAN'S BURDEN" (1897)

From Rudyard Kipling, *Rudyard Kipling's Verse* (New York: Doubleday, 1940), 321–23.

A student in this world history course once explained to me that "The White Man's Burden" made no sense because the phrase "white man's burden" meant something different to her from the way Kipling used the phrase. She read the text as if it came from her own time and place, exactly the wrong way to read a historical source. We read historical sources with an open mind to understand the perspective of the source, not to tell the source what it should or should not "really mean." This is the only way to fairly understand the past and the people of the past. Lessons or applications for the present can come only after the source has been interpreted on its own terms and in its own context.

This poem provides insights into the mentality of nineteenth-century imperialism. Kipling wrote the poem as a warning to the United States, the new imperial power. Kipling described the reaction he anticipated American colonists would receive from native people based on the experience he saw of the British in India and other colonies. In order to understand how Kipling saw his world, try to read the poem using the following general rule: every second-person reference is directed toward colonizing people and states (Americans). Third-person references refer to native people. Some references might seem counterintuitive, but do not let that deter you. Understand what Kipling said, and you can understand something of the mentality of his time. You might find it odd, for example, that a serf in the poem is a colonial rather than a native. In the way Kipling saw the universe, an enormous burden accompanies the responsibility of colonial powers to spread enlightenment. Thus, though we see today that native people in colonies were enslaved, enserfed, and brutalized, from Kipling's perspective, it was the colonials who suffered. He appears in this poem to believe colonials suffered for truth.

The White Man's Burden: The United States and the Philippine Islands

Take up the White Man's burden—
Send forth the best ye breed—
Go, bind your sons to exile
To serve your captives' need;
To wait, in heavy harness,
On fluttered folk and wild—
Your new-caught sullen peoples,
Half devil and half child.

Take up the White Man's burden—
In patience to abide,
To veil the threat of terror
And check the show of pride;

Take up the White Man's burden—
The savage wars of peace—
Fill full the mouth of Famine,

And bid the sickness cease;
And when your goal is nearest
(The end for others sought)
Watch sloth and heathen folly
Bring all your hope to nought.

Take up the White Man's burden—
No iron rule of kings,
But toil of serf and sweeper—
The tale of common things.
The ports ye shall not enter,
The roads ye shall not tread,
Go, make them with your living
And mark them with your dead.

Take up the White Man's burden,
And reap his old reward—
The blame of those ye better
The hate of those ye guard—
The cry of hosts ye humour
(Ah, slowly!) toward the light:—
"Why brought ye us from bondage,
Our loved Egyptian night?"

Take up the White Man's burden—
Ye dare not stoop to less—
Nor call too loud on Freedom
To cloak your weariness.
By all ye will or whisper,
By all ye leave or do,
The silent sullen peoples
Shall weigh your God and you.

Take up the White Man's burden!
Have done with childish days—
The lightly-proffered laurel,
The easy ungrudged praise:
Comes now, to search your manhood
Through all the thankless years,
Cold, edged with dear-bought wisdom,
The judgment of your peers.

—Rudyard Kipling

8. DECLARATION OF THE RIGHTS OF MAN AND OF THE CITIZEN (APPROVED BY THE NATIONAL ASSEMBLY OF FRANCE, AUGUST 26, 1789)

Prepared by Gerald Murphy. Distributed by the Cybercasting Services Division of the National Public Telecomputing Network (NPTN). Permission is hereby granted to download, reprint, and/or otherwise redistribute this file, provided appropriate point-of-origin credit is given to the preparer(s) and the National Public Telecomputing Network. http://www.constitution.org/fr/fr_drm.htm.

The following French declaration was one of the great political works of the French Revolution, which threw off the rule of kings (called the Old Regime or the ancien régime) and replaced it with a nation of citizens. The statement is one of the milestones in the history of humanism and stands today as a model for democratic societies.

The representatives of the French people, organized as a National Assembly, believing that the ignorance, neglect, or contempt of the rights of man are the sole cause of public calamities and of the corruption of governments, have determined to set forth in a solemn declaration the natural, unalienable, and sacred rights of man, in order that this declaration, being constantly before all the members of the Social body, shall remind them continually of their rights and duties; in order that the acts of the legislative power, as well as those of the executive power, may be compared at any moment with the objects and purposes of all political institutions and may thus be more respected, and, lastly, in order that the grievances of the citizens, based hereafter upon simple and incontestable principles, shall tend to the maintenance of the constitution and redound to the happiness of all.

Therefore the National Assembly recognizes and proclaims, in the presence and under the auspices of the Supreme Being, the following rights of man and of the citizen:

Articles:

1. Men are born and remain free and equal in rights. Social distinctions may be founded only upon the general good.
2. The aim of all political association is the preservation of the natural and imprescriptible rights of man. These rights are liberty, property, security, and resistance to oppression.
3. The principle of all sovereignty resides essentially in the nation. No body nor individual may exercise any authority which does not proceed directly from the nation.
4. Liberty consists in the freedom to do everything which injures no one else; hence the exercise of the natural rights of each man has no limits except those which assure to the other members of the society the enjoyment of the same rights. These limits can only be determined by law.
5. Law can only prohibit such actions as are hurtful to society. Nothing may be prevented which is not forbidden by law, and no one may be forced to do anything not provided for by law.

6. Law is the expression of the general will. Every citizen has a right to participate personally, or through his representative, in its foundation. It must be the same for all, whether it protects or punishes. All citizens, being equal in the eyes of the law, are equally eligible to all dignities and to all public positions and occupations, according to their abilities, and without distinction except that of their virtues and talents.

7. No person shall be accused, arrested, or imprisoned except in the cases and according to the forms prescribed by law. Any one soliciting, transmitting, executing, or causing to be executed, any arbitrary order, shall be punished. But any citizen summoned or arrested in virtue of the law shall submit without delay, as resistance constitutes an offense.

8. The law shall provide for such punishments only as are strictly and obviously necessary, and no one shall suffer punishment except it be legally inflicted in virtue of a law passed and promulgated before the commission of the offense.

9. As all persons are held innocent until they shall have been declared guilty, if arrest shall be deemed indispensable, all harshness not essential to the securing of the prisoner's person shall be severely repressed by law.

10. No one shall be disquieted on account of his opinions, including his religious views, provided their manifestation does not disturb the public order established by law.

11. The free communication of ideas and opinions is one of the most precious of the rights of man. Every citizen may, accordingly, speak, write, and print with freedom, but shall be responsible for such abuses of this freedom as shall be defined by law.

12. The security of the rights of man and of the citizen requires public military forces. These forces are, therefore, established for the good of all and not for the personal advantage of those to whom they shall be intrusted.

13. A common contribution is essential for the maintenance of the public forces and for the cost of administration. This should be equitably distributed among all the citizens in proportion to their means.

14. All the citizens have a right to decide, either personally or by their representatives, as to the necessity of the public contribution; to grant this freely; to know to what uses it is put; and to fix the proportion, the mode of assessment and of collection and the duration of the taxes.

15. Society has the right to require of every public agent an account of his administration.

16. A society in which the observance of the law is not assured, nor the separation of powers defined, has no constitution at all.

17. Since property is an inviolable and sacred right, no one shall be deprived thereof except where public necessity, legally determined, shall clearly demand it, and then only on condition that the owner shall have been previously and equitably indemnified.

9. AN AMERICAN SCIENTIST IN EARLY MEIJI JAPAN (1868–1912)

From Thomas C. Mendenhall, *An American Scientist in Early Meiji Japan* (Honolulu: University of Hawaii, 1989), 47–51. (Courtesy of Richard Rubinger.)

I think the distance from Tokyo to Fuji is about eighty miles and we traveled to the foot of the mountain by jinrikisha, arriving late at night, I remember, at the village of Tsubasheri (I am not sure of the spelling) [Subashiri], at which point the climbing is begun. We were to begin the ascent at 8 a.m. And all necessary arrangements for guides, carriers, etc., had been made for us in advance by our young men who had, by direction, preceded us by a day or two. The transportation of the tents and most of the equipage of the camp had been assigned to the students who went ahead, but Chaplin and I had decided to look after two of the most important instruments, those most likely to be injured by careless handling, ourselves.

I took charge of the break circuit chronometer and he of the transit instrument with which the chronometer rate was to be ascertained. We had two or three or four "go-riki," or strongmen, whose business it was to climb the mountain and carry freight, and these instruments were handed over to them when the ascent began. The transit, although broken up as much as seemed wise to diminish weight, furnished one package weighing 160 pounds, and I was astonished to see how comfortably one of our go-riki hoisted that upon his back and went his way upward, faster than we could go empty handed. Food was carried also, enough for several days, besides extra clothing, blankets, etc.

The ascent of the mountain was interesting and in places rather difficult. It was an all-day job but after passing the level of about six thousand feet near noon we came out above the line of tree growth and the views were very extended and fine. Perhaps one incident is worth recording.

On the night before there had passed through the village in which we were—sleeping there a few hours—a band of pilgrims who were to make the ascent of the mountain. The mountain has always been considered holy among the faithful Buddhists and Shintoists of Japan and pilgrimages to it are looked upon in very much the same light as are pilgrimages to Mecca among the people with whom I am now living temporarily. Every year bands of pilgrims were made up in various parts of the empire, numbering fifty to a hundred men and sometimes women and children and, under the direction of a leader, made the pilgrimage to the summit of Fujiyama and back, practically entirely afoot.

These men were dressed in white flowing garments, with immense hats of straw, like a small umbrella, and usually there was a flute or perhaps two or three in the party. The leader had a small bell with which he made signals governing the party when marching. Their garments, uniformly white, presented a curious appearance when we met them—and still more curious when we left them, owing the practice of stamping each pilgrim with the character or sign or cartouche of the shrine at which he had made his prayers. Every shrine was provided with a stamp, generally of wood, on which the character was cut, the size varying from one to five or six inches square. A pilgrim who had visited a shrine was anxious to have this stamp impressed on his garment (sometimes in black ink and sometimes in red) as a certificate which he might show to his friends at home of the fact that he had actually worshiped at this shrine. Of course only the most famous on the way had been thus visited, but the gowns of the pilgrims had already been used many times and some of them were pretty well covered. There are a number of shrines, or stations, eight in all I think, on the way up before the summit of the mountain is reached, and all of these must be properly endorsed upon the now rapidly disappearing white surface of the gown. The band of pilgrims (of which I am now writing—we saw many others afterward) had left the hotel earlier than we did and had not taken the same path or trail up the mountain that we took later, going somewhat out of the most direct way in order to pass certain shrines which our path left aside.

Before we had breakfast on the morning of our climb, I stepped out of the inn and looked toward the mountain. We had arrived sometime after dark on the night before and had not seen it nearby and hardly during the afternoon, as it was covered with clouds. But this morning was clear and the view of the great volcanic peak was most magnificent as I stood at its base on that morning—a sight I shall never forget, in fact. A few feet away from me I saw Chaplin also gazing at the mountain which rose before us, perfectly clear from clouds. Turning, he saw me and burst out with the exclamation, "My God, I don't wonder they worship it!"

Sometime near the middle of the afternoon we found ourselves greatly fatigued and, although we were now far above the timber line and really much more than halfway through our journey, the great peak of the mountain still looked to be as far away from us as at the start. We took frequent rests, lying down on the bare rock or powdered lava, and I confess that I began to feel a little discouraged and feared that my strength would not last long enough to get me to the top. Just then we were overtaken by the band of pilgrims I have referred to. We saw with interest the method of their work and almost unknown to ourselves we fell in with it and them and found great assistance and relief. We noted that the pilgrims were strictly under the orders of their leader and that he limited each effort to the taking of one hundred steps, which he counted in a loud voice. At the end of the group of one hundred steps, the pilgrims instantly fell to the ground, where they rested until called to their feet by the bell of the leader. What seemed to keep them in good spirits more than anything else was the repetition, in unison and with great rhythmic effect, of a simple phrase—"Ro-kun-sho-jo"—a short prayer in which they begged to be made clean in all their parts before they reached the summit of their desires. They kept step with this, not much regarding the leader's counting of the steps. This was a most excellent device which I have imitated many times since.

The thought of each pilgrim was not "Can I ever reach the top of this mountain," but rather, "I think I can take the next hundred steps," and he was aided in this by the rhythmic movement of the prayer and also by the fact that he did not even count the hundred steps himself —only kept going, knowing that he would not be obliged to go for long before there would be a lying-down spell. Thus he became for the time a mere machine, with no thought or worry about the magnitude of the task before him. We fell into the ways of this band, soon learned their prayer, repeating it with them and had their moral support during the remainder of our task.

I have already spoken of the pilgrimages made to the summit of Fujiyama, and to the shrines at which they stopped on the way up. The last of these shrines and the most important of all was on the summit, on the rim of the crater, a short distance from the station we had selected for our work. It was built with a good deal of care, out of selected fragments of lava, was about twenty feet long and perhaps eight feet wide and six to seven feet high. It had been built by pious priests and pilgrims many years ago, hundreds doubtless, and was very solid and strong. At it a priest remained during the pilgrimage season (the month of August) and it contained the sacred insignia of the Buddhist religion: the images of Buddha, the mirror, the "gohei" (strips of paper attached to a stick of wood), the sacred sword, etc., etc. There was a narrow doorway in front of which the pilgrims passed in bands, dropping on their knees in front of it, rubbing their hands together in prayer, and finally tossing in at the door a few coins (copper) as an offering to the god or to the priest.

The pilgrims usually spent only a very short time at the summit. Having spent the night at the eighth station, they returned to it, and even lower, before noon the day of their visit. I had more than once thought, as I wandered about trying to find some solution to our difficulty, of this small temple as a suitable place for conducting our experiments, but I had also thought that the priest in charge would not for a moment consider allowing it to be used for such a purpose. However, after finding that every other place must be abandoned, I at last determined to interview him and ascertain his attitude. As I had expected, he declined to consider such a proposition and seemed somewhat indignant at the idea of desecrating his shrine in that way. In a half hour I resolved to make another trial and this time I began by explaining to him (through one of my young men) the nature of the work in which we were engaged, telling him that if we were successful we would be able to compute the weight of the earth by means of the results of our experiments. I soon saw signs of interest in his face and, when I concluded by saying that we had been sent to do this work by the government at Tokyo, I was delighted to find him in a friendly attitude, and in a few moments he had yielded to us everything we asked, giving up his shrine for our exclusive use during the days necessary for our experiments.

We had began our preparations very promptly and vigorously and in a few hours all was ready. The image of Buddha and other insignia of worship had been removed from their places and packed in the rear end of the hut. The mountings for pendulums had been fixed upon stones projecting from the side of the wall; the chronograph had been mounted, connected with the chronometer, and set going; the astronomical transit had been mounted near the door of the hut, ready for star observations for rating the chronometer as soon as it should be dark enough.

The attitude of the pilgrims toward our work and the improvised observatory was interesting. Generally they continued to make their devotions before the door of the hut as at other shrines, often watching the slowly revolving chronographic cylinder with intense interest, thinking, as we learned, that it was some new-fashioned "praying machine" (praying machines were, and I suppose are still, quite common in Japan) and they threw their copper coins in at the door as had been done before. Each evening one of our young men would make quite a collection of these offerings and carry them to the priest.

On one of the days of our stay, when looking at a band of pilgrims approaching the summit, our attention was especially drawn to one of them, first because he was carrying a book in his hand and second because as he drew nearer we saw that he was a European in countenance, physique, etc. He proved to be a Jesuit priest, his book was the Bible. He lived with the natives, spoke their language fluently, and dressed, ate, and lived with them and as they did. He had come with them on this pilgrimage to study their habits and especially to make use of such opportunities as might offer themselves to do a little proselytizing. We invited him to lunch with us and found him a most intelligent and agreeable man.

On the fourth day we completed our work and fortunately, for just then there set a dense fog ending in rain which would have interfered most seriously with our operations. As it was, we were compelled to work very hard to get all of our things packed and ready for going down before the dense mist made it almost impossible to see an object ten feet away. Just before leaving the summit of the mountain I went again to the little temple or shrine in which we had carefully reestablished the insignia of Buddhist worship and, after thanking the priest who had permitted us to make use of it, I offered to give him money in compensation. I have forgotten just what I offered him, but it was to him a relatively large sum; to my surprise, however, he positively refused to accept anything, saying that he felt it to be an honor to be able to give some aid in the solution of such an interesting problem. I reported his generosity to the officials of the university, mentioned it in every official report and in public lectures given in many parts of the United States (in many of the largest cities) in which I have related the story of this experimental weighing of the earth.

I have always taken much pleasure in naming this liberal-minded Japanese, named Kinoshita, who allowed me to transform a holy shrine of almost the oldest of religions into a laboratory of modern science and to substitute for his sacred images the most recent devices for the accurate measure of time. I fancy that few priests of more civilized religions would have been equally accommodating.

10. LEO TOLSTOY, *THE KINGDOM OF GOD IS WITHIN YOU* (1894)

From Count Leo Tolstoy, *The Kingdom of God Is within You: Christianity Not as a Mystic Religion but as a New Theory of Life*, trans. Constance Garnett (New York: Cassell, 1894).

Leo Tolstoy is best known for his great novels, but he also wrote essays, some describing his Christian faith. This statement in particular shows Tolstoy's conviction that human civilization is of no lasting value, as the "kingdom of God" is the only goal worthy of attaining. Tolstoy argues here that Jesus commanded his followers to resist evil with good and to respond to violence with nonviolence.

The Kingdom of God Is within You: Christianity Not as a Mystic Religion but as a New Theory of Life

[p. 48] Did Christ really demand from his disciples that they should carry out what he taught them in the Sermon on the Mount? . . . can the Christian, or can he not, remaining a Christian, take part in the administration of government, using compulsion against his neighbors? And—the most important question hanging over the heads of all of us in these days of universal military service—can the Christian, or can he not, remaining a Christian, against Christ's direct prohibition, promise obedience in future actions directly opposed to his teaching? And can he, by taking his share of service in the army, prepare himself to murder men and even actually murder them?

[p. 67] The foreign freethinking critics have tried in a delicate manner, without being offensive to me, to give the impression that my conviction that mankind could be guided by such a naive doctrine as that of the Sermon on the Mount proceeds from two causes: that such a conviction is partly due to my want of knowledge, my ignorance of history, my ignorance of all the vain attempts to apply the principles of the Sermon on the Mount to life, which have been made in history and have led to nothing; and partly it is due to my failing to appreciate the full value of the lofty civilization to which mankind has attained at present, with its Krupp cannons, smokeless powder, colonization of Africa, Irish Coercion Bill, parliamentary government, journalism, strikes, and the Eiffel Tower.

[pp. 342–43] . . . people . . . who think to make men advance by means of external force . . . say that the Christian life cannot be established without the use of violence, because there are savage races outside the pale of Christian societies in Africa and in Asia (there are some who even represent the Chinese as a danger to civilization), and that in the midst of Christian societies there are savage, corrupt, and, according to the new theory of heredity, congenital criminals. And violence, they say, is necessary to keep savages and criminals from annihilating our civilization.

But these savages within and without Christian society, who are such a terror to us, have never been subjugated by violence, and are not subjugated by it now. Nations have never subjugated other nations by violence alone. If a nation which subjugated another was on a lower level of civilization, it has never happened that it succeeded in introducing its organization of life by violence. On the contrary, it was always forced to adopt the organization of life existing in the conquered nation. If ever any of the nations conquered by force have been really subjugated or even nearly so, it has always been by the action of public opinion, and never by violence, which only tends to drive a people to further rebellion.

[pp. 478–88] But it is not even this question "What will happen?" that agitates men when they hesitate to fulfill the Master's will. They are troubled by the question how to live without those habitual conditions of life which we call civilization, culture, art, and science. We feel ourselves all the burdensomeness of life as it is; we see also that this organization of life must inevitably be our ruin, if it continues. At the same time we want the conditions of our life which arise out of this organization—our civilization, culture, art, and science—to remain intact.

Nowadays, after so many centuries of fruitless efforts to make our life secure by the pagan organization of life, it must be evident to everyone that all efforts in that direction only introduce fresh dangers into personal and social life, and do not render it more secure in any way.

Whatever names we dignify ourselves with, whatever uniforms we wear, whatever priests we anoint ourselves before, however many millions we possess, however many guards are stationed along our road, however many policemen guard our wealth, however many so-called criminals, revolutionists, and anarchists we punish, whatever exploits we have performed, whatever states we may have founded, fortresses and towers we may have erected—from Babel to the Eiffel Tower—there are two inevitable conditions of life, confronting all of us, which destroy its whole meaning: (1) death, which may at any moment pounce upon each of us; and (2) the transitoriness of all our works, which so soon pass away and leave no trace.

Whatever we may do—found companies, build palaces and monuments, write songs and poems—it is all not for long time. Soon it passes away, leaving no trace. And therefore, however we may conceal it from ourselves, we cannot help seeing that the significance of our life cannot lie in our personal fleshly existence, the prey of incurable suffering and inevitable death, not in any social institution or organization. Whoever you may be who are reading these lines, think of your position and of your duties—not of your position as landowner, merchant, judge, emperor, president, minister, priest, laid on you by those positions, but of your real positions in eternity as a creature who at the will of Someone has been called out of unconsciousness after an eternity of non-existence to which you may return at any moment at his will. Think of your duties—not your supposed duties as a landowner to your estate, as a merchant to your business, as emperor, minister, or official to the state, but of your real duties, the duties that follow from your real position as a being called into life and endowed with reason and love.

Are you doing what he demands of you who has sent you into the world, and to whom you will soon return? Are you doing what he wills? Are you doing his will, when as landowner or manufacturer you rob the poor of the fruits of their toil, basing your life on this plunder of the workers, or when, as judge or governor, you ill treat men, sentence them to execution, or when as soldiers you prepare for war, kill and plunder?

Share all that you have with others, do not heap up riches, do not steal, do not cause suffering, do not kill, do not unto others what you would not they should do unto you, all that has been said not eighteen hundred, but five thousand years ago, and there could be no doubt of the truth of this law if it were not for hypocrisy. Except for hypocrisy men could not have failed, if not to put the law in practice, at least to recognize it, and admit that it is wrong not to put it in practice.

Your duties as a citizen cannot but be subordinated to the superior obligations of the eternal life of God, and cannot be in opposition to them. As Christ's disciples said eighteen centuries ago: "Whether it be right in the sight of God to hearken unto you more than unto God, judge ye" (Acts iv. 19); and, "We ought to obey God rather than men" (Acts v. 29).

It is asserted that, in order that the unstable order of things, established in one corner of the world for a few men, may not be destroyed, you ought to commit acts of violence which destroy the eternal and immutable order established by God and by reason. Can that possibly be?

"But seek ye first the kingdom of God, and his righteousness, and all these things shall be added unto you" (Matt vi. 33).

The sole meaning of life is to serve humanity by contributing to the establishment of the kingdom of God, which can only be done by the recognition and profession of the truth by every man.

"The kingdom of God cometh not with outward show; neither shall they say, Lo here! or, Lo there! for behold, the kingdom of God is within you" (Luke xvii. 20, 21).

11. CONFUCIUS (CIRCA 551–479 BCE)

From Zhong Yong, "The Doctrine of the Mean," trans. James Legge, in *The Chinese Classics*, vol. 1 (Hong Kong: Hong Kong University Press, 1960); and "The Mandate of Heaven," trans. James Legge, in *The Sacred Books of China: The Texts of Confucianism*, ed. F. Max Mueller, vol. 3 of *The Sacred Books of the East* (Oxford: Clarendon Press, 1879–1910), 9295.

Included are selections describing two influential Confucian concepts. "The Doctrine of the Mean" and "The Mandate of Heaven" describe concepts of state, individual, society, and religion that span more than two thousand years and still today represent active mentalities in all aspects of Chinese and east Asian societies.

"The Mandate of Heaven" describes a political and social philosophy that served as the Chinese explanation for the success or failure of dynasties down to the end of the empire in 1912. When a dynasty fell, the reason offered by China's sages was that it had lost the moral right to rule, which is given by Heaven alone. In this context, heaven did not mean a personal god but a cosmic, all-pervading power.

The Doctrine of the Mean

[1] What Heaven has conferred is called The Nature; an accordance with this nature is called The Path of duty; the regulation of this path is called Instruction.

The path may not be left for an instant. If it could be left, it would not be the path. On this account, the superior man does not wait till he sees things, to be cautious, nor till he hears things, to be apprehensive.

There is nothing more visible than what is secret, and nothing more manifest than what is minute. Therefore the superior man is watchful over himself, when he is alone.

While there are no stirrings of pleasure, anger, sorrow, or joy, the mind may be said to be in the state of Equilibrium. When those feelings have been stirred, and they act in their due degree, there ensues what may be called the state of Harmony. This Equilibrium is the great root from which grow all the human actings in the world, and this Harmony is the universal path which they all should pursue. Let the states of equilibrium and harmony exist in perfection, and a happy order will prevail throughout heaven and earth, and all things will be nourished and flourish. . . .

[4] The Master said, "I know how it is that the path of the Mean is not walked in:—The knowing go beyond it, and the stupid do not come up to it. I know how it is that the path of the Mean is not understood: The men of talents and virtue go beyond it, and the worthless do not come up to it. . . ."

[11] The Master [Confucius] said, "To live in obscurity, and yet practice wonders, in order to be mentioned with honor in future ages: this is what I do not do. . . .

[13] ". . . When one cultivates to the utmost the principles of his nature, and exercises them on the principle of reciprocity, he is not far from the path. What you do not like when done to yourself, do not do to others. . . ."

[14] The superior man does what is proper to the station in which he is; he does not desire to go beyond this.

In a position of wealth and honor, he does what is proper to a position of wealth and honor. In a poor and low position, he does what is proper to a poor and low position. Situated among barbarous tribes, he does what is proper to a situation among barbarous tribes. In a position of sorrow and difficulty, he does what is proper to a position of sorrow and difficulty. The superior man can find himself in no situation in which he is not himself.

In a high situation, he does not treat with contempt his inferiors. In a low situation, he does not court the favor of his superiors. He rectifies himself, and seeks for nothing from others, so that he has no dissatisfactions. He does not murmur against Heaven, nor grumble against men.

Thus it is that the superior man is quiet and calm, waiting for the appointments of Heaven, while the mean man walks in dangerous paths, looking for lucky occurrences.

The Master said, "In archery we have something like the way of the superior man. When the archer misses the center of the target, he turns round and seeks for the cause of his failure in himself."

[15] The way of the superior man may be compared to what takes place in traveling, when to go to a distance we must first traverse the space that is near, and in ascending a height, when we must begin from the lower ground.

It is said in the Book of Poetry, "Happy union with wife and children is like the music of lutes and harps. When there is concord among brethren, the harmony is delightful and enduring. Thus may you regulate your family, and enjoy the pleasure of your wife and children. . . ."

[16] ". . . Thus it is that Heaven, in the production of things, is sure to be bountiful to them, according to their qualities. Hence the tree that is flourishing, it nourishes, while that which is ready to fall, it overthrows. . . ."

[19] ". . . By means of the ceremonies of the ancestral temple, they distinguished the royal kindred according to their order of descent. By ordering the parties present according to their rank, they distinguished the more noble and the less. By the arrangement of the services, they made a distinction of talents and worth. In the ceremony of general pledging, the inferiors presented the cup to their superiors, and thus something was given the lowest to do. At the concluding feast, places were given according to the hair, and thus was made the distinction of years.

"They occupied the places of their forefathers, practiced their ceremonies, and performed their music. They reverenced those whom they honored, and loved those whom they regarded with affection. Thus they served the dead as they would have served them alive; they served the departed as they would have served them had they been continued among them.

"By the ceremonies of the sacrifices to Heaven and Earth they served God, and by the ceremonies of the ancestral temple they sacrificed to their ancestors. He who understands the ceremonies of the sacrifices to Heaven and Earth, and the meaning of the several sacrifices to ancestors, would find the government of a kingdom as easy as to look into his palm!"

[20] The Duke Ai asked about government. The Master said, " . . . the administration of government lies in getting proper men. Such men are to be got by means of the ruler's own character. That character is to be cultivated by his treading in the

ways of duty. And the treading those ways of duty is to be cultivated by the cherishing of benevolence.

"Benevolence is the characteristic element of humanity, and the great exercise of it is in loving relatives. Righteousness is the accordance of actions with what is right, and the great exercise of it is in honoring the worthy. The decreasing measures of the love due to relatives, and the steps in the honor due to the worthy, are produced by the principle of propriety. . . .

"Some are born with the knowledge of those duties; some know them by study; and some acquire the knowledge after a painful feeling of their ignorance. But the knowledge being possessed, it comes to the same thing. Some practice them with a natural ease; some from a desire for their advantages; and some by strenuous effort. But the achievement being made, it comes to the same thing."

". . . When those in inferior situations do not obtain the confidence of the sovereign, they cannot succeed in governing the people. There is a way to obtain the confidence of the sovereign; if one is not trusted by his friends, he will not get the confidence of his sovereign. There is a way to being trusted by one's friends; if one is not obedient to his parents, he will not be true to friends. There is a way to being obedient to one's parents; if one, on turning his thoughts in upon himself, finds a want of sincerity, he will not be obedient to his parents. There is a way to the attainment of sincerity in one's self; if a man do not understand what is good, he will not attain sincerity in himself.

"Sincerity is the way of Heaven. The attainment of sincerity is the way of men. He who possesses sincerity is he who, without an effort, hits what is right, and apprehends, without the exercise of thought: he is the sage who naturally and easily embodies the right way. He who attains to sincerity is he who chooses what is good, and firmly holds it fast.

"To this attainment there are requisite the extensive study of what is good, accurate inquiry about it, careful reflection on it, the clear discrimination of it, and the earnest practice of it. . . ."

The Mandate of Heaven

In the twelfth month of the first year . . . Yi Yin sacrificed to the former king, and presented the heir-king reverently before the shrine of his grandfather. All the princes from the domain of the nobles and the royal domain were present; all the officers also, each continuing to discharge his particular duties, were there to receive the orders of the chief minister. Yi Yin then clearly described the complete virtue of the Meritorious Ancestor for the instruction of the young king.

He said, "Oh! of old the former kings of Xia cultivated earnestly their virtue, and then there were no calamities from Heaven. The spirits of the hills and rivers alike were all in tranquility; and the birds and beasts, the fishes and tortoises, all enjoyed their existence according to their nature. But their descendant did not follow their example, and great Heaven sent down calamities, employing the agency of our ruler—who was in possession of its favoring appointment. The attack on Xia may be traced to the orgies in Ming Tiao. . . . Our king of Shang brilliantly displayed his sagely prowess; for oppression he substituted his generous gentleness; and the millions of the people gave him their hearts. Now your Majesty is entering on the inheritance of his virtue;—all depends on how you commence your reign. To set up love, it is for you to love your relations; to set up respect, it is for you to respect your elders. The commencement is in the family and the state. . . .

"Oh! the former king began with careful attention to the bonds that hold men together. He listened to expostulation, and did not seek to resist it; he conformed to the wisdom of the ancients; occupying the highest position, he displayed intelligence; occupying an inferior position, he displayed his loyalty; he allowed the good qualities of the men whom he employed and did not seek that they should have every talent. . . .

"He extensively sought out wise men, who should be helpful to you, his descendant and heir. He laid down the punishments for officers, and warned those who were in authority, saying, 'If you dare to have constant dancing in your palaces, and drunken singing in your chambers,—that is called the fashion of sorcerers; if you dare to see your hearts on wealth and women, and abandon yourselves to wandering about or to the chase,—that is called the fashion of extravagance; if you dare to despise sage words, to resist the loyal and upright, to put far from you the aged and virtuous, and to seek the company of . . . youths,—that is called the fashion of disorder. Now if a high noble or officer be addicted to one of these three fashions with their ten evil ways, his family will surely come to ruin; if the prince of a country be so addicted, his state will surely come to ruin. The minister who does not try to correct such vices in the sovereign shall be punished with branding.' . . .

"Oh! do you, who now succeed to the throne, revere these warnings in your person. Think of them!—sacred counsels of vast importance, admirable words forcibly set forth! The ways of Heaven are not invariable:—on the good-doer it sends down all blessings, and on the evil-doer it sends down all miseries. Do you but be virtuous, be it in small things or in large, and the myriad regions will have cause for rejoicing. If you not be virtuous, be it in large things or in small, it will bring the ruin of your ancestral temple."

12. BILL CLINTON ON GLOBALIZATION (2004)

Edited by Elizabeth Carter, Robert J. Dole Institute of Politics. By permission, "Liz," Bill Clinton Institute, New York, NY, September 2004.

This text is a selection from a speech presented by Bill Clinton to his friend and colleague Senator Bob Dole. Clinton's statement provides a president's perspective on globalization and the global problems facing the world and the United States.

DATE: May 21, 2004
EVENT: First Annual Dole Lecture
FEATURED SPEAKER: President Bill Clinton
LOCATION: Allen Field House, University of Kansas

[Following an introduction by Bob Dole and statements by Bill Clinton] . . .
Now, I say that to try to drive this point home. You may agree or disagree with our policy in Iraq. You may think, for example, we should have put more emphasis in Afghanistan, where the Al Qaida are, because they're the ones that caused 9/11. But—[Applause] Wait, wait, wait. This is thinking time, not cheering time. You can cheer later if you like it. But think. The point I wish to make is this. You should have disagreements with your leaders and your colleagues, but if it becomes immediately a question of questioning people's motives, and if immediately you decide that somebody who sees a whole new situation differently than you must be a bad person and somehow twisted inside, we are not going to get very far in forming a more perfect union. Now, why does it happen? Here's why. Because at the end of the Cold War, the paradigm, the way we looked at the world evaporated and we had to create a new one. It was my great good fortune, but also challenge, to become the first president to serve my entire term in the post–Cold War era, to be the first president of the 21st century, as well as the last president of the 20th century. America is in one of those periods where we are trying to come to grips with fundamental questions. How are we going to relate to globalization, how are we going to relate to the global threat on terror? What is the role of government in our lives now? What are we to make of all this new diversity? Is it going to—the religious and racial and ethnic diversity—is it going to make us more fractured or will it make us more interesting and more unified? These are big, big questions.

When the Cold War was over and the industrial age began to be replaced by an information age, ever more globalized, we changed the way we work, the way we live, the way we relate to each other and certainly the way we relate to the rest of the world in ways that are marvelous and ways that are frightening. I believe we live in an age normally referred to as globalization, sometimes referred to as the global information society. I prefer the term "interdependence." Because it goes far beyond economics. There's good and bad in it. I have a cousin that lives in the hills of Northwest Arkansas that plays chess over the Internet with a guy in Australia twice a week. They take turns figuring out who's got to stay up late. On the other hand, 9/11 was a testimony to the power of interdependence. Don't you agree? The Al Qaida, what did they do? They used open borders, easy travel, easy access to information and technology to turn an airplane into a weapon of mass destruction, to murder 3,100 people nearly, in Washington, Pennsylvania, and New York from 70 countries. It's a story of global interdependence. The dark side of global interdependence. When I was president, 30% of the economic growth that we had came from trade.

When I was president, Senator Dole was always pushing me until we got it right—to end the ethnic slaughter in Bosnia. A hundred years ago, we wouldn't have known how to find Bosnia on a map. But it offended us because we had to watch those people being killed just because they were Muslims being slaughtered, and because we wanted Europe to be united and peaceful and democratic for the first time in history, to make the Cold War all worthwhile. So then we would be united, we'd be working together, we'd be fighting the problems of the rest of the world together. That, too, is interdependence. So if it can be positive or negative, it's obvious what we ought to be doing. If you agree with me. We need a strategy that builds up the positive and beats down the negative. We need to recognize that interdependence is inherently an unstable condition. And we need to move the world toward a more integrated, global community defined by three things, shared benefits, shared responsibilities, and shared values. That's what I believe.

Now—[Applause] Here's the point I want to make. This may seem simple to you, but if everybody thought that way, then in every area, there would be a slightly liberal or a slightly conservative way to do that, and then we would have all these debates, and in all probability, as free discussion usually does, it would lead to the best possible outcome. I'll just give you an example. In my view, there are five big issues here, for whatever it's worth. Number one, we have to have a strategy to fight the new security threats of terror and weapons of mass destruction that is both offensive and defensive. What's the best way to have homeland defense? If you have limited amount of money, if you think about it like this, then you can say, well, I think what we should do is triple or quadruple the number of containers we're checking at the ports and airports for biological or chemical weapons or somebody else can say, no, I think we should be reinforcing the bridges or putting guards outside the electrical plants that have nuclear power or whatever you think. But the point is, if you're focused on it that way, you can focus on homeland defense. What's the best way to pursue an offensive strategy? Is it to go to Iraq and establish a beach head of freedom in the Middle East or is it to stay in Afghanistan and root out the Al Qaida, and then turn your attention to the rest of the world? But once you're focused on it, you can have a civilized debate, and if you both agree on the issue, then just because somebody has got a different idea than you do about how to handle it, you don't think there's something wrong with them.

So that's the first thing. Second thing we have to do is to have a strategy to make a world with more partners and fewer terrorists. Now, why do I say that? Besides the fact that I'm a Democrat. Why would I say that? Why should every American think that? Even people that don't believe in social programs? Because if you believe the world is interdependent and you cannot kill, occupy, or imprison all your actual or potential adversaries, sooner or later you have to make a deal. That's what politics is. If there's a factual matter, that's what I talked until I was blue in the face in the Middle East about, they walked away from that peace deal in 2000. It was the dumbest thing I've ever seen in my life. All we've got now is the Middle East is not a bit less interdependent today than it was when we made seven years of progress toward peace. We got 3,000 dead Palestinians, about 9,200 dead—I mean 920 dead Israelis. They're no less interdependent. Nothing has changed except more people are dead and now more people are mad and there's less trust and it's harder to deal with it, but they are not a bit less interdependent. So you remember that. If you're in any environment in life that you don't have total control over, you have to make a deal. That's what politics is. And that's why compromise is honorable, not dishonorable.

[Applause]

So, anyway, so how would you go about making a world with more friends than fewer enemies? Well, first of all, you gotta realize that half the people that live on earth aren't part of this globalized economy that works. On earth, half the people live on less than $2 a day, of the 6 billion people on earth, 1 billion live on less than $1 a day, a billion and a half people never get a clean glass of water, a billion people go to bed hungry every night, 10 million kids die of preventable childhood diseases, and one in four deaths every year on earth now come from AIDS, TB, malaria, and infections related to diarrhea. Most of them are little children who never got a single clean glass of water in their lives. So for a tiny fraction of what we spend on defense and homeland defense, and I do mean tiny, we could double what we spend to help put all the children in the world who aren't in school in school, to pay our fair share of the fight against the world's diseases—[Applause]—and to do these other things. And to give you an example, after 9/11, I think we increased—believe this is right. I think we increased defense and homeland defense 60 something billion dollars in one year. We could double our assistance programs in these other areas, double them, for about 10 or 12. In a budget that must now be nearly $2 trillion, I don't know what it is. I haven't looked at it. I don't have to look at it anymore, so I don't, but I think that's about what it is. So you got to have a strategy for terror, a strategy for more friends.

The third thing I think is to find more ways to cooperate institutionally. This is a big challenge for America because we're going through a period in history when we have unrivaled military, economic, and political power. So every time we make a deal with anybody to do anything, we're giving up some of our freedom of action. Maybe a good deal for them, not a good deal for us because most of the time we can do whatever we please. The problem is, we will not be the only military, economic, and political superpower forever. If present growth rates continue, China, India, and the European Union will equal or surpass the United States sometime in the 21st century, just because of their size. They may not ever have to reach the per capita income we do to have greater output. So I think we should do that, but if you believe that, then it puts a whole different cast on the debates you hear today over putting up missile defense, getting rid of the anti-ballistic missile treaty, should we be part of the comprehensive treaty, should we be part of the criminal court, should we be part of the Kyoto Climate Change Accord, and I say that, I didn't join—there's one I didn't join. I didn't join the land mine treaty because they wrote it in a way that was absolutely hostile to the United States, and we have the finest record of any country in the world in promoting demining in the last 15 years, and it had enormous bipartisan support. Bob supported it. And so I'm not saying we can join every treaty, but I'm saying we should have a preference for being part of every conceivable network that will bring people together, because I can tell you something. It's just like any club you belong to, any organization you belong to, it builds the habit of working with other people. And the more you're in the habit of believing that if you stay on the team, good things will happen, as compared to if you get off the team, the more likely we are to find peace and resolution to the problems of the 21st century.

So I think that's very, very important and now I want to make just two more points. So terror, more friends, more cooperation. Fourth thing is, we have to keep making America better. A lot of our influence in the world comes not from the size of our military or our arsenal of weapons, but from the power of our example. One of the schools that was destroyed in New York City on September 11th, 2001, the children had to leave and go meet in a temporary facility. So Hillary and I went to this school to see these kids, elementary school kids. Six hundred kids from over 80 different national, racial, and ethnic groups. One school. If we can prove that freedom brings mutual respect and that people can be proud of their heritage and proud of their religion, and proud of everything that's special and still bound together in a more perfect union, that will do as much to undermine the long-term appeal of terror as anything else we can do. Just continuing to prove America works.

[Applause]

. . . But anyway, none of this will happen until we move the American people's way of thinking about other people forward. And let me explain what I mean by that. You guys love your basketball team. I like the Arkansas Razorbacks. We're all pulling for different people in the NBA playoffs. We have wars you know who you're for— you got over 600 people from Kansas in Iraq today putting their lives on the line. We think in categories that are oppositional. And we have to organize ourselves in little boxes. I see a man, I see a woman, I see somebody that's white, I see somebody that's black, I see somebody that's brown, all right. I see a Baptist, a Catholic, a Jew, a Muslim, a Buddhist, a Sikh. I mean, if we couldn't put ourselves in boxes, nobody could function. You think about how many University courses are designed to giving people more boxes to think with. . . . But at some point it has to become irrelevant. The whole story of humanity is a story of forming a more perfect union. Ever since our forebearers stood up on the African savanna, something over 100,000 years ago, they learned to relate to other people, first they were in clans. Then larger tribes, then villages, and they would come into contact with wider and wider circles of people that had different views and felt threatened, and there would be fighting and killing, but sooner or later, before they destroyed the human race, they'd find a way to get along. In the twentieth century, our weapons were so powerful, we nearly got it wrong. But we escaped. We gave in to neither the tyranny of Hitler or the tyranny of communism or the power of our weapons to destroy. We threaded a big needle there. And everybody that made a contribution deserves our gratitude. But the point I want to make is that if you believe to go back to the founders that our job is to form a more perfect union and nobody has got the whole truth, then everybody's got a contribution to make. And I think America, if we're ever going to truly defeat terror without changing the character of our own country or compromising the future of our children, has got to not only say, "Okay, I want to shoulder my responsibilities, I want to create my share of opportunities" but we have to find a way to define the future in terms of a humanity that goes beyond our country, that goes beyond any particular race, that goes beyond any particular religion. We should continue to judge people based on what they do. And if they persist in terror, we should punish them. We should go to war, we should use military power, we should do whatever we have to do. I'm not suggesting we act like it doesn't matter what you do. It matters a great deal what you do. But we have to be able to say to the world, we want a home for every peaceable person. We like our faith, we like our ethnic group, we like our crowd, we like our basketball team, we like the way it is. But there's a place for you here, too.

The world has never before, never in all of human history, had to do this. It's a big psychological jump. It's easy for somebody like me, who has been to 100 and something countries to stand up and give a speech like this. It's quite a different thing for a country to live this way. It was not until 1945, after World War II, that we even had a United Nations. The Americans thought it was weird. The Senate defeated it after World War I. "Who wants to be in a United Nations with all those guys? You gotta be kidding." So then we nearly blow ourselves up and we have a U.N., right? And a universal declaration of human rights. It was a fraud until the end of the Cold War. Not a fraud, we just couldn't make it available to everybody. We have had 15 short years since 1989 to build a global community in which everybody thinks, like Dole does, that people in Kosovo and people in Kansas are more alike than they are different.

Now, I will leave you with one last statistic to put in your little box. My last year in the White House, Hillary sponsored a lot of these what we call "Millennium Evenings." We'd bring in people to talk about big questions. One night, Vinton Cerf, who sent the first e-mail to his profoundly deaf wife, now 22 years ago, and Eric Ladner, a biologist and genome expert from Harvard, came to talk about how the digital chip made possible the sequencing of the human genome. Forget about that. You know the most interesting thing that he said? Genetically, all human beings are more than 99.9% identical,[1] and the genetic differences among individuals within a given racial group are larger than the genetic differences of one group as compared to another. Now, next time you start to feel like you really need to demonize somebody, think about that. Biggest laugh I ever got at the State of the Union Address was telling the Republicans and the Democrats whether they liked it or not, they were 99.9% the same. There had been a lot of blood spread over that one-tenth of one percent, and all you really have to do is figure out how to free yourself to live by the other 99.9%. Thank you very much.

[Applause]

---

1. Researchers now set this number slightly lower, closer to 99.0 percent.

13. WE ARE NOT MONKEYS, WE ARE HUMAN BEINGS (JUNE 2002)

From Hashem Aghajari, "From Monkey to Man," accessed October 2004, http://iranian.com/Opinion/2002/December/Aghajari. English translation reprinted courtesy of the publisher.

For this speech, professor of history Hashem Aghajari was arrested, jailed, and sentenced to beating, internal banishment, and death.

The Protestant movement wanted to rescue Christianity from the clergy and the Church hierarchy. . . . We [Muslims] do not need mediators between us and God. We do not need mediators to understand God's holy books. The Prophet [Jesus] spoke to the people directly? We don't need to go to the clergy; each person is his own clergy. . . .

The Role of the Traditional Clerics

At the time of the Constitutional Revolution [1905–1907], the Islamic clergy was opposed to modern sciences such as chemistry and physics. [In their eyes], chemistry meant that there is no God. But in today's world the clerics take what suits them. If I drive a Peykan [a cheap Iranian-made car] they drive the latest model luxury cars [audience applause]. Is this right?

They have made these concessions because they use [modernity for their own benefit]; they taste it and then decide that it isn't such a bad thing. Seventy or 80 years ago, they opposed these things in the name of Islam; they called it Haraam [forbidden in Islam]. Up until very recently, learning English in Islamic religious institutes of higher learning was forbidden.

. . . In our tradition, Shi'ites wear a ring on the middle finger of the left hand. This is a symbol of being a Muslim. If you ask one of these clerics, they say it is an obligation and a religious principle. Look at the writings of Alameh Majlesi and the book of Halieh Al-Motaqin—the book that guided Muslims 1,400 years ago. Now imagine that today a Muslim wants to dress like they did then, eat like they used to, act like they used to. Is this Islam?

. . . [The way in which] the religious scholars of previous generations understood and interpreted Islam is not Islam. It was their interpretation of Islam; [however,] just as they had the right to interpret the Koran [in their way], we have the same right. Their interpretation of Islam is not an article of faith for us. . . . For years, young people were afraid to open a Koran. They said, "We must go ask the Mullahs what the Koran says," [since] it was used primarily in mosques and cemeteries. The new generation was not allowed to come near the Koran; [young people] were told that [first] they needed [training in] 101 methods of thought and they did not possess them. Consequently, [the young people] feared reading the Koran. Then came Shariati, and he told the young people that these ideas were bankrupt; [he said] you could understand the Koran using your own methods—you could understand as well as the religious leaders who claim to have a ton of knowledge. The religious leaders taught that if you understand the Koran on your own, you have committed a crime. They feared that their racket would cease to exist if young people learned [the Koran] on their own. . . .

A Cleric Is Not a Divine Being

Shariati used to say that the relationship between [the clergy] and the people should be like the relationship between teacher and pupil—not between leader and follower, not between icon and imitator; the people are not monkeys who merely imitate. The pupils understand and react, and they try to expand their own understanding, so that someday they will not need the teacher. The relationship that the fundamentalist religious people [seek] is one of master and follower; the master must always remain master and the follower will always remain follower. This is like shackles around the neck [i.e., eternal slavery]. . . .

Non-Muslims Too Have Inalienable Rights

If we, as Muslims of divine and perfect Islam, value mankind, and say that [people] are human beings regardless of religion, even if they are not Muslims, even if they are not Iranians, such as Turks, Kurds and Lurs, whatever they may be—[we should say that] they are human and they have inalienable rights. Dr. Shariati believed that in the Western world, humanism is not strongly rooted because it is not based on religious principles. But in Islam, humanism is God's creation; it is by God's grace that we are here. These should not be merely nice words that we utter, like saying people have rights. Such words are vitally important—they are crowns on our heads. [Therefore], when [ordinary people] want to express an opinion, [the clerics cannot say] they haven't the power to decide and don't know what's good for them.

Today's Islam [should be] "core Islam," not "traditional Islam." Islamic Protestantism is logical, practical and humanist. It is thoughtful and progressive. . . . We need a religion that respects the rights of all—a progressive religion, rather than a traditional religion that tramples the people. We cannot say "Anyone who is not with me is against me." One can be whatever one wants to be. One must be a good person, a pure person. We must not say that if you are not with us we can do whatever we want to you. By behaving as we do, we are trampling our own religious principles. . . .

A Call for Islamic Humanism and Islamic Protestantism

Today, more than ever, we need the "Islamic humanism" and "Islamic Protestantism" that Dr. Shariati advocated. Today, we need it more than ever. While [the leaders] of the Islamic Republic apparently do not recognize human rights, this principle has been recognized by our constitution. In many non-Islamic countries, they at least recognize these principles in dealing with their own people. Maybe when it comes to other people, they oppress them—[like] what Bush is doing, and most Western nations, if they had the power.

Human rights have become so vital in some foreign countries that some of our own clergy, whom I see going for two or three weeks of medical treatment, become enchanted with how the authorities of those countries act towards their own people. About 150 years ago, [a Muslim cleric] went to Europe; when he came back, he said, "I saw no Muslims in Europe, but I saw Islam" [i.e., he saw righteousness]. In our time, we see Muslims, but we don't see Islam. [APPLAUSE]

Without Respect for Human Beings, There Is No Islam

The regime divides people into insiders and outsiders. They [the ruling clergy] can do whatever they want to the outsiders. They can go to their homes, steal their property, slander them, terrorize them, and kill them—like [the intellectual activists] Said Hejjarian, and the late [Dariush] Forouhar and his wife [Parvaneh Eskandari]—because they were outsiders. Is this Islamic logic? When there is no respect for human beings? When [Imam] 'Ali [the Prophet Muhammad's son-in-law and successor, according to Shi'ite Islam] sent an emissary to Egypt, he told him, "You are a powerful man. Be good and just to the people. There are two groups of these people: Either they are Muslims, and therefore your brothers, or they are your fellow human beings. Behave towards them according to Islam." Islam does not say Muslims and non-Muslims . . . [VOICES FROM THE AUDIENCE] Someone shouts: "Because one fatwa is the word of the Koran and the other is not." Someone else protests, calling "Aghajari namard" (you are not a man, therefore you are a scoundrel), and repeats, "You are a liar," "namard," and "You accuse God and the prophets of lying." [AT THIS POINT, AGHAJARI LEAVES THE MEETING.]

Iran, June 2002

14. *DOCUMENTS ON THE EXPULSION OF THE GERMANS FROM EASTERN-CENTRAL EUROPE* (1945–1950)

From "The Expulsion of German Populations from Czechoslovakia," in *Documents on the Expulsion of the Germans from East-Central Europe*, vol. 4, ed. Theodor Schieder, trans. G. H. Sausmarez et al. (Bonn: Federal Ministry for Expellees, Refugees, and War Victims, and Gerhard Rautenberg, Ostfriesland, 1960), 351, 390.

These selections are taken from multiple volumes containing hundreds of similar accounts. The testimonies were collected after the end of the Second World War, from survivors of the mass expulsions of millions of German residents of the "Eastern Zones" from 1945 until 1952.

No. 12. Report of the Experiences of Dr. August Karl Lassmann, Wholesale Merchant, of Troppau

[The author describes how, after trying to escape the Red Army, he found himself back in Red Army territory, hiding out in a factory yard.]

In this way, the first days passed relatively calmly for us, whilst in the houses of the inner town, women and girls were violated and raped every night by Russian soldiers. Especially where the Russians found alcohol, they could not be kept away from the women and it mattered very little of what age they were. A lot of evil and many tragedies have happened in this respect—although our small group was not directly affected.

No. 29. Report of the Experiences of Kurt Schmidt, Civil Engineer of Brunn

On 5 May 1945 . . . Czech guerrillas interned me with my family—my wife and three small children below the age of six. Together with some 300 other Germans, mostly women and children who were evacuees or refugees from Silesia, we were kept prisoners for the subsequent days in a former orphanage in Pribram. . . . It took three days before we got a once-daily ration of soup; no bread was issued during these first days. . . . After 9 May, when the Soviet troops marched in, [this] maltreatment got even worse. After dark the women especially were exposed to the greatest danger. We were not allowed to lock the rooms in the internment camps and the keys had been taken away. Supported by the Czechs, the Russians came and took what they wanted, using the necessary brutal force. In a neighboring camp, located in the former technical school, a woman did not want to submit to the Russians—she was thrown from the third floor into the yard. In the same camp, a woman who had children with her, was raped until she was dead. (I had this information confirmed by several inmates.) Four of the women who had been taken during the night by Russians from the camp, never returned. Those who did return were so broken in spirit that their only wish was to die. All this happened next to us and in countless cases. . . .

[He and those with him were then moved to a different camp.] Hunger and death ruled in the camp. We were even more forcibly reminded of death by the executions which took place in full public view inside the camp. Any SS member who was discovered in the camp, was killed in public. One day, six youths were beaten until they lay motionless, water was poured over them (which the German women had to fetch) and then the beating continued till there was no sign of life left. The terribly mutilated bodies were deliberately exhibited for several days next to the latrine. A 14-year-old boy was shot together with his parents because it was alleged that he had tried to stab a Revolutionary Guard with a pair of scissors. These are only some of the examples of the executions which took place almost daily, mostly by shooting. Apart from the death penalty, there was corporal punishment, mainly carried out in the room of the commandant of the Revolutionary Guard. Women too were beaten with a whip on their naked bodies, for instance the woman leader of a trek who had somewhat delayed a report.

15. DOCUMENTS OF HUMANITY (1945-1950)

From K. O. Kurth, Helen Taubert, and Margaret Brooke, *Documents of Humanity during the Mass Expulsions* (Göttingen: Göttingen Research Committee, 1952), 91, 22, 31, 106.

Two Young Men in Civilian Clothes

I was on the railway station at Eberswalde, which is on the Stettin-Berlin line. The station was full of people who camped on the platforms for never ending days. In the night I was frightened out of my sleep by girls screaming and crying wildly. Not a man moved, it would have been no good. During the next day an old man with his young daughter turned up and we sat next to each other, they were on the way home, to Berlin. Then came two young men in civilian clothes. We talked together and it was two young French boys who had come from Gubinnen and Insterburg. They sat the girl between them. They advised me most urgently not to try and get back to East Prussia, as many did do, poor things. On the next day we went different ways, looking for a chance of getting to Berlin. Then I saw them, on a freight train, the girl between the two Frenchmen, the father beside them. They waved and I waved back.

    —Signed, Anna Muehlich

A Colored American

Around April 1945 we were in a school in Koenigshof, in Czechoslovakia, when the order came to evacuate because the Russians were drawing near. We started at 2 o'clock in the morning, in the dark, each going as best he could. As I could not walk very far, because I am already 70 years old, I had to stay behind. My niece, with her little boy of six and three other women, left me. Then a car full of soldiers came and took us along. We got as far as a crossing where we were to turn off to the Pilsen camp, and the car was stopped by American soldiers, and we had to get out, there was a discussion, and the car turned back. We then learned that the soldiers who had picked us up were Russian officers who were carrying us off [to kill them]. We then had to go farther on foot. It was afternoon and about four o'clock, and all the others had long since gone on. I had taken my shoes off and was walking in my stocking feet, but I could not go on and sat down at the roadside with my bag and thought I must just leave myself in the hands of the Lord. It was not long before a Czech came by on a bicycle and took away my bag and left me with just my purse. After awhile an American negro soldier, with a gun slung over his shoulder, came towards me and I thought my end had come. He came straight up to me and said, "Now Ma, can't you get along." "No," I replied. He took my hand and helped me to get up, put on my shoes, and then gave me his arm to help me along. We went a little way and came to a village where there was an inn. He put me on a bench under the trees, because he wanted to go and have something to eat. He soon came back with a cup of coffee with sugar and cream and a buttered roll and said, "Now get your strength up again and then we'll go on, I patrol as far as the [border]." He told me that in America he had an old mother whom he perhaps would never see again, and I told him about my husband who is dead and my only son who became a prisoner in Russia in 1944 and about whom I have, till now, had no news at all.

—Signed, Frau Anna Guenther

With the Red Cross

I was head of the Red Cross centre at the railway station in Komotau, Sudetenland, during the terrible May of 1945, and in the months that followed. . . . Should sober-minded readers not find the experiences described here to be very heroic, I must stress that any assistance given to Germans by a foreigner meant going against either a Russian or a Czech order, and that the punishment for this was severe. . . . One day I received the terrible order that no more soup was to be served to German civilians or sick or wounded German soldiers, only to foreigners and children under six. If I did not comply with this order I could expect to be shot. The result was, of course, that a lot of soup was left over, which I was then ordered to throw away, while the poor creatures were collapsing from hunger. I can still see this misery before me if I close my eyes, and again it was the prisoners [freed prisoners of war, formerly held by the German army], who got me to give them soup and then discreetly hid the cans in the washrooms of the Red Cross, indicating them to the starving refugees with a fleeting glance. A thankful look, a stealthy grasp of the hand was their reward. I shall never forget how my oldest assistant often spoke to the English PWs [prisoners of war], asking them to spend the night in the nurses' home, so as to protect the German girls who were regarded as fair game by Russians and Czechs. She never met with refusal . . .

These few notes are all the more valuable if one remembers that those who helped us did so out of humanity and without the least thought of personal advantage.

—Signed, Marie Konwalinka

On a Station in Czechoslovakia

At Station X, in Czechoslovakia, our freight train had been standing for three days in the burning sun. We had no food, although we did have water. Anyone who risked going to the village to try and buy food came back beaten up and robbed of everything. The freight cars were guarded by young Czechs who thought it great fun to shoot off their guns in the air, and laughed cynically when the children screamed or the women jumped with fright. . . . My husband and I and our three children sat sadly around a little fire. A handsome man behind us said, "If you will make my soup for me I can lend you a saucepan." We got talking together and our new friend was a Pole, an interpreter. He had been interned in Germany [he was a POW] but was not filled with hatred against the Germans. I shall never forget what he said to us, the sense of which was, "the victors are not those wild, revengeful, pillaging people who are passing us now, full of the power they are already misusing, the victors are probably you and I, who in such a chaos are good neighbors and try to represent our nations and mankind worthily in the simple things in life."

—Signed [illegible]

16. PILGRIMS ON FU-JI (1879)

From Mrs. Julia D. Carrothers, *The Sunrise Kingdom: Life Scenes in Japan* (Philadelphia: Presbyterian Board of Publishing, 1879), 146–52.

Note: Earlier transliterations of the name "Fuji" called for a hyphen, as in the following text.

A motley crowd had assembled at the entrance of the hotel when our travelers left Ka-ko-ne to return to Tokio. Ka-go-men, pilgrims, travelers, drivers with their pack-horses—all were congregated there. Those bound for Tokio went down the mountain on its eastern slope, while the pilgrims turned their faces westward toward Fu-ji. Let us follow them.

They went up the one steep street of Ha-ko-ne, out of the gate through which the old daimios passed, and just outside of which some old idols stood, as if keeping guard in the place of sentinels.

Under grand old trees, between mossy banks from which hung tangled masses of vines and ivy, and where ferns grew in rank profusion and fair white lilies bloomed, went the pilgrims stepping from rock to rock and stopping to quench their thirst at some cooling spring. At noon they halted for dinner at Mi-shi-ma, a large town at the foot of the western side of Ha-ko-ne.

Just opposite the hotel was a large temple, and back of the temple a beautiful grove. Pretty winding walks under the shady trees, with thatched cottages and people walking to and fro, made the place very charming. But the most attractive object at Mi-shi-ma was the stream which the pilgrims passed as they went out of town. Down from the mountain it came, pure and fresh, and in such volume that it was sufficient to quench the thirst of all the people of Mi-shi-ma through all time. Truly, Japan is a well-watered country—"a land of brooks of water, of fountains and depths, that spring out of valleys and hills, and these bright waters flow over a green, sunny land. It is strange how earth's most lovely regions are the ones most defiled by sin. Even Sodom and Gomorrah stood in the plain of Jordan which was like the garden of the lord."

At Yo-shi-wa-ra, a large town near the base of Fu-ji, the pilgrims passed the night. Everywhere they performed their devotions, going for this purpose into all the large temples. And now they came to the mountain.

Fu-ji is an extinct volcano, which stands by itself in the centre of a large plain. It rises (taking the average of several estimates) thirteen thousand feet above the level of the sea, being the highest point of elevation in Japan. Perpetual snow lies upon the summit. Its cone is made of cinders, and is one of the most symmetrical in the world. It is the steepest of all volcanoes, the angle being forty-five degrees. Its ashes cause at a distance the peculiar purple hue which distinguishes the mountain. A hundred years have elapsed since the last eruption.

As the pilgrims started on their journey in the early morning their way lay for a time over a plain whereon beautiful flowers grew. Beginning the ascent, they passed through a grove of cedars, then through a field of flowers, where the vegetation was rank, and then reached hut No. 1. At nearly regular intervals on the mountain are these places of refuge for the pilgrims. . . . There are eight or nine of these huts and without their shelter travel on the mountain would be almost impossible.

. . . Then began the real ascent of the cinderstone. It all looked black and desolate. Vegetation suddenly ceased, with the exception of a few patches of a sickly green shrub, and the feet of the pilgrims sank deep into the ashes at every step. The way was strewn with castoff sandals . . . they wear out quickly on Fu-ji. . . .

After reaching No. 6, the way up to the crater became yet more steep and difficult, and the scenery of the mountain the very extreme of desolateness. On went the pilgrims, toiling slowly upward, purposing to sleep at the crater. Large stones impeded their progress, and their feet sank deeper and deeper into the cinders. The air became so rarified that it failed to satisfy their lungs, and breathing became difficult. . . . The ashes, flying up at every step, made the throats of the pilgrims very dry, so they constantly wanted to drink.

At last they stood on the summit. A priest sat by the side of a deep well, constructed no one knows how long ago, and a most remarkable feature in such a scene—a well of water at the very crater's mouth. He pulled the buckets up and down by a rope on a windlass, and as the cold, sparkling water came, he gave it to the weary, thirsty pilgrims. How interesting and deeply suggestive this incident, though happening in a heathen land and in a false pagan worship! There is the counterfeit, and there is the true. Can we doubt where the true well is, and the real water of life?

The pilgrims, refreshed, went on to worship at the crater. Around the deep, yawning pit were the idols of wood and stone, similar to those in their temples and homes. All was quiet.

17. INDUSTRIAL MANCHESTER (1844) AND THE CONDITIONS OF WOMEN WORKING IN THE ENGLISH MINES (1842)

From Friedrich Engels, *The Condition of the Working-Class in England in 1844* (London: Swan Sonnenschein, 1892), 45, 48, 53.

The whole assemblage of buildings is commonly called Manchester, and contains about four hundred thousand inhabitants, rather more than less. The town itself is peculiarly built, so that a person may live in it for years, and go in and out daily without coming into contact with a working-people's quarter or even with workers, that is, so long as he confines himself to his business or to pleasure walks. This arises chiefly from the fact, that by unconscious tacit agreement, as well as with outspoken conscious determination, the working-people's quarters are sharply separated from the sections of the city reserved for the middle-class. . . .

I may mention just here that the mills almost all adjoin the rivers or the different canals that ramify throughout the city, before I proceed at once to describe the labouring quarters. First of all, there is the old town of Manchester, which lies between the northern boundary of the commercial district and the Irk. Here the streets, even the better ones, are narrow and winding, as Todd Street, Long Millgate, Withy Grove, and Shude Hill, the houses dirty, old, and tumble-down, and the construction of the side streets utterly horrible. Going from the Old Church to Long Millgate, the stroller has at once a row of old-fashioned houses at the right, of which not one has kept its original level; these are remnants of the old pre-manufacturing Manchester, whose former inhabitants have removed with their descendants into better built districts, and have left the houses, which were not good enough for them, to a population strongly mixed with Irish blood. Here one is in an almost undisguised working-men's quarter, for even the shops and beer houses hardly take the trouble to exhibit a trifling degree of cleanliness. But all this is nothing in comparison with the courts and lanes which lie behind, to which access can be gained only through covered passages, in which no two human beings can pass at the same time. Of the irregular cramming together of dwellings in ways which defy all rational plan, of the tangle in which they are crowded literally one upon the other, it is impossible to convey an idea. And it is not the buildings surviving from the old times of Manchester which are to blame for this; the confusion has only recently reached its height when every scrap of space left by the old way of building has been filled up and patched over until not a foot of land is left to be further occupied.

The south bank of the Irk is here very steep and between fifteen and thirty feet high. On this declivitous hillside there are planted three rows of houses, of which the lowest rise directly out of the river, while the front walls of the highest stand on the crest of the hill in Long Millgate. Among them are mills on the river, in short, the method of construction is as crowded and disorderly here as in the lower part of Long Millgate. Right and left a multitude of covered passages lead from the main street into numerous courts, and he who turns in thither gets into a filth and disgusting grime, the equal of which is not to be found—especially in the courts which lead down to the Irk, and which contain unqualifiedly the most horrible dwellings which I have yet beheld. In one of these courts there stands directly at the entrance, at the end of the covered passage, a privy without a door, so dirty that the inhabitants can pass into and out of the court only by passing through foul pools of stagnant urine and excrement. This is the first court on the Irk above Ducie Bridge—in case any one should care to look into it. Below it on the river there are several tanneries which fill the whole neighbourhood with the stench of animal putrefaction. Below Ducie Bridge the only entrance to most of the houses is by means of narrow, dirty stairs and over heaps of refuse and filth. The first court below Ducie Bridge, known as Allen's Court, was in such a state at the time of the cholera that the sanitary police ordered it evacuated, swept, and disinfected with chloride of lime. Dr. Kay gives a terrible description of the state of this court at that time. Since then, it seems to have been partially torn away and rebuilt; at least looking down from Ducie Bridge, the passer-by sees several ruined walls and heaps of debris with some newer houses. The view from this bridge, mercifully concealed from mortals of small stature by a parapet as high as a man, is characteristic for the whole district. At the bottom flows, or rather stagnates, the Irk, a narrow, coal-black, foul-smelling stream, full of debris and refuse, which it deposits on the shallower right bank.

In dry weather, a long string of the most disgusting, blackish-green, slime pools are left standing on this bank, from the depths of which bubbles of miasmatic gas constantly arise and give forth a stench unendurable even on the bridge forty or fifty feet above the surface of the stream. But besides this, the stream itself is checked every few paces by high weirs, behind which slime and refuse accumulate and rot in thick masses. Above the bridge are tanneries, bone mills, and gasworks, from which all drains and refuse find their way into the Irk, which receives further the contents of all the neighbouring sewers and privies. It may be easily imagined, therefore, what sort of residue the stream deposits. Below the bridge you look upon the piles of debris, the refuse, filth, and offal from the courts on the steep left bank; here each house is packed close behind its neighbour and a piece of each is visible, all black, smoky, crumbling, ancient, with broken panes and window frames. The background is furnished by old barrack-like factory buildings. On the lower right bank stands a long row of houses and mills; the second house being a ruin without a roof, piled with debris; the third stands so low that the lowest floor is uninhabitable, and therefore without windows or doors. Here the background embraces the pauper burial-ground, the station of the Liverpool and Leeds railway, and, in the rear of this, the Workhouse, the "Poor-Law Bastille" of Manchester, which, like a citadel, looks threateningly down from behind its high walls and parapets on the hilltop, upon the working-people's quarter below.

. . . Here, as in most of the working-men's quarters of Manchester, the pork-raisers rent the courts and build pig-pens in them. In almost every court one or even several such pens may be found, into which the inhabitants of the court throw all refuse and offal, whence the swine grow fat; and the atmosphere, confined on all four sides, is utterly corrupted by putrefying animal and vegetable substances. . . .

Such is the Old Town of Manchester, and on re-reading my description, I am forced to admit that instead of being exaggerated, it is far from black enough to convey a true impression of the filth, ruin, and uninhabitableness, the defiance of all considerations of cleanliness, ventilation, and health which characterise the construction of this single district, containing at least twenty to thirty thousand inhabitants. And such a district exists in the heart of the second city of England, the first manufacturing city of the world. If any one wishes to see in how little space a human being can move, how little air—and such air!—he can breathe, how little of civilisation he may share and yet live, it is only necessary to travel hither. True, this is the Old Town, and the people of Manchester emphasise the fact whenever any one mentions to them the frightful condition of this Hell upon Earth; but what does that prove? Everything which here arouses horror and indignation is of recent origin, belongs to the industrial epoch.

Women Miners in the English Coal Pits (1842)

Great Britain, Parliamentary Papers, 1842, vol. 16, pp. 2, 196. Thanks to the *History Source-book*, Fordham University, halsall@murray.fordham.edu, http://www.fordham.edu/Halsall/mod/1842womenminers.asp.

In England, exclusive of Wales, it is only in some of the colliery districts of Yorkshire and Lancashire that female Children of tender age and young and adult women are allowed to descend into the coal mines and regularly to perform the same kinds of underground work, and to work for the same number of hours, as boys and men; but in the East of Scotland their employment in the pits is general; and in South Wales it is not uncommon.

West Riding of Yorkshire: Southern Part—in many of the collieries in this district, as far as relates to the underground employment, there is no distinction of sex, but the labour is distributed indifferently among both sexes, except that it is comparatively rare for the women to hew or get the coals, although there are numerous instances in which they regularly perform even this work. In great numbers of the coalpits in this district the men work in a state of perfect nakedness, and are in this state assisted in their labour by females of all ages, from girls of six years old to women of twenty-one, these females being themselves quite naked down to the waist.

"Girls," says the Sub-Commissioner [J. C. Symons], —regularly perform all of the various offices of trapping, hurrying [Yorkshire terms for drawing the loaded coal corves], filling, riddling, tipping, and occasionally getting, just as they are performed by boys. One of the most disgusting sights I have ever seen was that of young females, dressed like boys in trousers, crawling on all fours, with belts round their waists and chains passing between their legs, at day pits at Hunshelf Bank, and in many small pits near Holmfirth and New Mills: it exists also in several other places. I visited the Hunshelf Colliery on the 18th of January: it is a day pit; that is, there is no shaft or descent; the gate or entrance is at the side of a bank, and nearly horizontal. The gate was not more than a yard high, and in some places not above 2 feet.

When I arrived at the board or workings of the pit I found at one of the side-boards down a narrow passage a girl of fourteen years of age in boy's clothes, picking down the coal with the regular pick used by the men. She was half sitting half lying at her work, and said she found it tired her very much, and "of course she didn't like it." The place where she was at work was not two feet high. Further on were men lying on their sides and getting. No less than six girls out of eighteen men and children were employed in this pit.

Whilst I was in the pit the Rev Mr Bruce, of Wadsley, and the Rev Mr Nelson, of Rotherham, who accompanied me, and remained outside, saw another girl of ten years of age, also dressed in boys clothes, who was employed in hurrying, and these gentlemen saw her at work. She was a nice-looking little child, but of course as black as a tinker, and with a little necklace round her throat.

In two other pits in the Huddersfield Union I have seen the same sight. One year in New Mills, the chain, passing high up between the legs, had worn large holes in their trousers; and any sight more disgustingly indecent or revolting can scarcely be imagined than these girls at work—no brothel can beat it.

On descending Messrs Hopwood's pit at Barnsley, I found assembled round a fire a group of men, boys, and girls, some of whom were at the age of puberty; the girls as well as boys stark naked down to the waist, their hair bound up with a tight cap and trousers supported by their hips. (At Silkstone and at Flockton they were in their shifts and trousers.) Their sex was recognizable only by their breasts, and some little difficulty occasionally arose in pointing out to me which were girls and which were boys, and which caused a good deal of laughing and joking. In the Flockton and Thornhill pits the system is even more indecent: for though the girls are clothed, at least three-fourths of the men for whom they "hurry" work stark naked, or with a flannel waist coat only, and in this state they assist one another to fill the corves 18 or 20 times a day: I have seen this done myself frequently.

When it is remembered that these girls hurry chiefly for men who are not their parents; that they go from 15 to 20 times a day into a dark chamber (the bank face), which is often 50 yards apart from any one, to a man working naked, or next to naked, it is not to be supposed but that where opportunity thus prevails sexual vices are a common occurrence. Add this to the free intercourse, and the rendezvous at the shaft or bullstake, where the corves are brought, and consider the language to which the young ear is habituated, the absence of religious instruction, and the early age at which contamination begins, and you will have before you, in the coal-pits where females are employed, the picture of a nursery for juvenile vice which you will go far and we above ground to equal.

Two Women Miners (1842)

Betty Harris, age 37: I was married at 23, and went into colliery when I was married. I used to weave when I was about 12 years old; can neither read nor write. I work for Andrew Knowles, of Little Bolton (Lancs), and make sometimes 7s a week, sometimes not so much. I am a drawer, and work from 6 in the morning to 6 at night. Stop about an hour at noon to eat my dinner; have bread and butter for dinner; I get no drink. I have two children, but they are too young to work. I worked at drawing when I was in the family way. I know a woman who has gone home and washed herself, taken to her bed, delivered a child, and gone to work again under the week.

I have a belt around my waist, and a chain passing between my legs, and I go on my hands and feet. The road is very steep, and we have to hold by a rope; and when there is no rope, by anything we can catch hold of. There are six women and about six boys and girls in the pit I work in; it is very hard work for a woman. The pit is very wet where I work, and the water comes over our clog-tops always, and I have seen it up to my thighs; it rains in at the roof terribly. My clothes are wet through almost all day long. I was never ill in my life, but when I was lying in.

My cousin looks after my children in the day time. I am very tired when I get home at night; I fall asleep sometimes before I get washed. I am not so strong as I was, and cannot stand my work so well as I used to. I have drawn till I have bathe skin off me; the belt and chain is worse when we are in the family way. My feller (husband) has beaten me many a times for not being ready. I were not used to it at first, and he had little patience.

I have known many a man beat his drawer. I have known men take liberties with the drawers, and some of the women have bastards.

Patience Kershaw, age 17, Halifax: I go to a pit at 5 o'clock in the morning and come out at 5 in the evening; I get my breakfast, porridge and milk, first; I take my dinner with me, a cake, and eat it as I go; I do not stop or rest at any time for the purpose, I get nothing else until I get home, and then I have potatoes and meat, not every day meat.

18. REPORT OF THE NATIONAL INTELLIGENCE COUNCIL'S 2020 PROJECT

From National Intelligence Council, *Mapping the Global Future: Report of the National Intelligence Council's 2020 Project*, accessed January 29, 2015, http://www.dni.gov/files/documents/Global%20Trends_Mapping%20the%20Global%20Future%202020%20Project.pdf.

Executive Summary

At no time since the formation of the Western alliance system in 1949 have the shape and nature of international alignments been in such a state of flux. The end of the Cold War shifted the tectonic plates, but the repercussions from these momentous events are still unfolding. Emerging powers in Asia, retrenchment in Eurasia, a roiling Middle East, and transatlantic divisions are among the issues that have only come to a head in recent years. The very magnitude and speed of change resulting from a globalizing world—apart from its precise character—will be a defining feature of the world out to 2020. Other significant characteristics include: the rise of new powers, new challenges to governance, and a more pervasive sense of insecurity, including terrorism. As we map the future, the prospects for increasing global prosperity and the limited likelihood of great power conflict provide an overall favorable environment for coping with what are otherwise daunting challenges. The role of the United States will be an important variable in how the world is shaped, influencing the path that states and nonstate actors choose to follow.

New Global Players

The likely emergence of China and India, as well as others, as new major global players—similar to the advent of a united Germany in the 19th century and a powerful United States in the early 20th century—will transform the geopolitical landscape, with impacts potentially as dramatic as those in the previous two centuries. In the same way that commentators refer to the 1900s as the "American Century," the 21st century may be seen as the time when Asia, led by China and India, comes into its own. A combination of sustained high economic growth, expanding military capabilities, and large populations will be at the root of the expected rapid rise in economic and political power for both countries.

Most forecasts indicate that by 2020 China's gross national product (GNP) will exceed that of individual Western economic powers except for the United States. India's GNP will have overtaken or be on the threshold of overtaking European economies.

Because of the sheer size of China's and India's populations—projected by the US Census Bureau to be 1.4 billion and almost 1.3 billion respectively by 2020—their standard of living need not approach Western levels for these countries to become important economic powers.

Barring an abrupt reversal of the process of globalization or any major upheavals in these countries, the rise of these new powers is a virtual certainty. Yet how China and India exercise their growing power and whether they relate cooperatively or competitively to other powers in the international system are key uncertainties. The economies of other developing countries, such as Brazil, could surpass all but the largest European countries by 2020; Indonesia's economy could also approach the economies of individual European countries by 2020.

By most measures—market size, single currency, highly skilled work force, stable democratic governments, and unified trade bloc—an enlarged Europe will be able to increase its weight on the international scene. Europe's strength could be in providing a model of global and regional governance to the rising powers. But aging populations and shrinking work forces in most countries will have an important impact on the continent. Either European countries adapt their work forces, reform their social welfare, education, and tax systems, and accommodate growing immigrant populations (chiefly from Muslim countries), or they face a period of protracted economic stasis.

With these and other new global actors, how we mentally map the world in 2020 will change radically. The "arriviste" powers—China, India, and perhaps others such as Brazil and Indonesia—have the potential to render obsolete the old categories of East and West, North and South, aligned and nonaligned, developed and developing. Traditional geographic groupings will increasingly lose salience in international relations. A state-bound world and a world of mega-cities, linked by flows of telecommunications, trade and finance, will co-exist. Competition for allegiances will be more open, less fixed than in the past.

Impact of Globalization

We see globalization—growing interconnectedness reflected in the expanded flows of information, technology, capital, goods, services, and people throughout the world—as an overarching "mega-trend," a force so ubiquitous that it will substantially shape all the other major trends in the world of 2020. But the future of globalization is not fixed; states and nonstate actors—including both private companies and NGOs—will struggle to shape its contours. Some aspects of globalization—such as the growing global interconnectedness stemming from the information technology (IT) revolution—almost certainly will be irreversible. Yet it is also possible, although unlikely, that the process of globalization could be slowed or even stopped, just as the era of globalization in the late 19th and early 20th centuries was reversed by catastrophic war and global depression.

19. TWO ARTICLES ON THE DISCOVERIES AT BLOMBOS CAVE (2002)

National Science Foundation, "Abstract Engravings Show Modern Behavior Emerged Earlier Than Previously Thought" news release, January 10, 2002. By permission, Chris Henshilwood, African Heritage Research Institute, Centre for Development Studies, University of Bergen, Bergen, Norway.

I. Origins of Modern Human Behaviour: The Debate

The origins of anatomically modern people (*Homo sapiens*) almost certainly lie in Africa at about 300,000–150,000 years ago and genetic evidence shows that all living people are related to these African ancestors. . . . Evidence emerging from a few recently excavated African sites is beginning to change the picture. One of these sites, Blombos Cave, located in the southern Cape, South Africa, contains excellently preserved Middle Stone Age (MSA) deposits that date to older than 70,000 years. Excavations at this site between 1992–2000 have yielded remarkable, yet anomalous finds that are directly relevant to the modern human behaviour debate. These finds include a range of bone tools, finely crafted bifacial stone points, an engraved bone fragment and evidence for modern subsistence practices including fishing.

II. Abstract Engravings Show Modern Behavior Emerged Earlier Than Previously Thought

People were able to think abstractly, and accordingly behave as modern humans much earlier than previously thought, according to a paper appearing in this week's issue of *Science*.

Christopher Henshilwood, professor at the University of Bergen, Norway, adjunct professor at the State University of New York, Stony Brook, and the Iziko-South African Museum in Cape Town and his team found abstract representations of two pieces of ochre, two and three inches long. The objects, dated to at least 70,000 years ago, were recovered from the Middle Stone Age layers at Blombos Cave, a site on the southern Cape shore of the Indian Ocean 180 miles east of Cape Town, South Africa. Henshilwood's work at the cave is supported by the National Science Foundation (NSF).

The earliest previous evidence of abstract representations is from the Eurasian Upper Paleolithic period mainly in France and dated to less than 35,000 years ago. Ochre, a form of iron ore, is frequently found in stone age sites less than 100,000 years old and may have been used symbolically as a body or decorative paint and possibly also for skin protection and tanning animals' hides.

Rather than being outlines of animals or other representations drawn from nature, the designs on the two pieces of ochre show a consistent representation of the development of arbitrary conventions to express mutually understood concepts. "They may have been constructed with symbolic intent, the meaning of which is now unknown," Henshilwood said. "These finds demonstrate that ochre use in the Middle Stone Age was not exclusively utilitarian and, arguably, the transmission and sharing of the meaning of the engravings relied on fully syntactical language," he added. The two pieces of ochre were first scraped and ground to create flat surfaces. They were then marked with cross hatches and lines to create a consistent complex geometric motif. The discovery adds important new insights to understanding the development of humans, who are known to have been anatomically modern in Africa about 100,000 years ago.

20. CODE OF HAMMURABI (SELECTED LAWS) (CIRCA 1780 BCE)

The Code of Hammurabi, trans. L. W. King, annotated by Charles F. Horne, accessed July 5, 2002, gopher://gopher.vt.edu:10010/11.

Many relics of Hammurabi's reign (1795–1750 BCE) have been preserved. . . . The most remarkable of the Hammurabi records is his code of laws, the earliest-known example of a ruler proclaiming publicly to his people an entire body of laws, arranged in orderly groups, so that all men might read and know what was required of them. The code was carved upon a black stone monument, eight feet high, and clearly intended to be . . . in public view. This noted stone was found in the year 1901, not in Babylon, but in a city of the Persian mountains, to which some later conqueror must have carried it in triumph. It begins and ends with addresses to the gods.

. . .

15. If any one take a male or female slave of the court, or a male or female slave of a freed man, outside the city gates, he shall be put to death.

16. If any one receive into his house a runaway male or female slave of the court, or of a freedman, and does not bring it out at the public proclamation of the major domus, the master of the house shall be put to death.

. . .

53. If any one be too lazy to keep his dam in proper condition, and does not so keep it; if then the dam break and all the fields be flooded, then shall he in whose dam the break occurred be sold for money, and the money shall replace the corn which he has caused to be ruined.

. . .

108. If a tavern-keeper (feminine) does not accept corn according to gross weight in payment of drink, but takes money, and the price of the drink is less than that of the corn, she shall be convicted and thrown into the water.

109. If conspirators meet in the house of a tavern-keeper, and these conspirators are not captured and delivered to the court, the tavern-keeper shall be put to death.

110. If a "sister of a god" open a tavern, or enter a tavern to drink, then shall this woman be burned to death.

. . .

129. If a man's wife be surprised with another man, both shall be tied and thrown into the water, but the husband may pardon his wife and the king his slaves.

130. If a man violate the wife (betrothed or child-wife) of another man, who has never known a man, and still lives in her father's house, and sleep with her and be surprised, this man shall be put to death, but the wife is blameless.

131. If a man bring a charge against one's wife, but she is not surprised with another man, she must take an oath and then may return to her house.

132. If the "finger is pointed" at a man's wife about another man, but she is not caught sleeping with the other man, she shall jump into the river for her husband.

. . . .

138. If a man wishes to separate from his wife who has borne him no children, he shall give her the amount of her purchase money and the dowry which she brought from her father's house, and let her go.

. . .

141. If a man's wife, who lives in his house, wishes to leave it, plunges into debt, tries to ruin her house, neglects her husband, and is judicially convicted: if her husband offer her release, she may go on her way, and he gives her nothing as a gift of release. If her husband does not wish to release her, and if he take another wife, she shall remain as servant in her husband's house.

142. If a woman quarrel with her husband, and say: "You are not congenial to me," the reasons for her prejudice must be presented. If she is guiltless, and there is no fault on her part, but he leaves and neglects her, then no guilt attaches to this woman, she shall take her dowry and go back to her father's house.

143. If she is not innocent, but leaves her husband, and ruins her house, neglecting her husband, this woman shall be cast into the water.

. . .

195. If a son strike his father, his hands shall be hewn off.

196. If a man put out the eye of another man, his eye shall be put out.

197. If he break another man's bone, his bone shall be broken.

198. If he put out the eye of a freed man, or break the bone of a freed man, he shall pay one gold mina.

199. If he put out the eye of a man's slave, or break the bone of a man's slave, he shall pay one-half of its value.

200. If a man knock out the teeth of his equal, his teeth shall be knocked out.

201. If he knock out the teeth of a freed man, he shall pay one-third of a gold mina.

[Conclusion:] The king who rules among the kings of the cities am I. My words are well considered; there is no wisdom like unto mine. By the command of Shamash, the great judge of heaven and earth, let righteousness go forth in the land: by the order of Marduk, my lord, let no destruction befall my monument. In E-Sagil, which I love, let my name be ever repeated; let the oppressed, who has a case at law, come and stand before this my image as king of righteousness; let him read the inscription, and understand my precious words: the inscription will explain his case to him; he will find out what is just, and his heart will be glad, so that he will say: "Hammurabi is a ruler, who is as a father to his subjects, who holds the words of Marduk in reverence, who has achieved conquest for Marduk over the north and south, who rejoices the heart of Marduk, his lord, who has bestowed benefits for ever and ever on his subjects, and has established order in the land."

21. THE *MAHABHARATA* (BEFORE 1000 BCE)

From The Sister Nivedita (Margaret E. Noble) of Ramakrishna-Vivekananda and Ananda K. Coomaraswamy, *Myths of the Hindus and Buddhists* (London: Harrap, 1913), 118–21.

How the Princes Learned to Shoot

Now Bhishma, the royal grandsire, became eager to find for the princes of the two imperial houses a teacher who might train them thoroughly in the use of arms. And it happened one day about this time that the boys, all in a company, were playing at ball in the forests outside Hastinapura, when their ball rolled away from them and fell into an old well. Try as they would, there was not one of them who could get it back. All kinds of efforts were made by each in turn, but without avail. It seemed as if the ball would never be recovered. Just when their boyish anxiety and vexation were at their height, their glances fell, with one accord, on a Brahman sitting near whom they had not at first noticed. He was thin and dark of hue, and appeared to be resting after the performance of his daily worship. "Oh Brahman!" cried the lads, surrounding him in a body, "can you show us how to recover our ball?" The Brahman smiled a little and said: "What? What? Scions of the royal house, and you don't shoot well enough for that! If only you'll promise me my dinner, I will bring up not only your ball but also this ring, which I now throw down, by means of a few blades of grass." And suiting the action to the word, he took a ring off his own finger and threw it into the well. "Why, Brahman-ji, we'll make you rich for life," cried one of the lads, "if you can really do as you say."

"Is it so?" said the Brahman. "Then look at this grass," and he plucked a handful of long grass growing near. "I am able by a spell to give to this grass a virtue that weapons might not have. Behold, here I throw"; and as he spoke he took aim and threw a single blade of grass with such deftness and precision that it pierced the ball that lay in the well as if it had been a needle. Then throwing another blade, he pierced the first, and so on and so on, till he had a chain of grass, by which it was easy to draw up the ball.

By this time the interest of the boys was centered more on the skill of the Brahman than on the recovery of their plaything, and they exclaimed with one accord: "The ring, too, O Brahman! Show us how you can recover the ring!"

The Recovery of the Ring

Then Drona—for that was the name of the Brahman—took up his bow, which had been lying beside him, and selecting an arrow from the quiver that he wore, he shot it into the well, and the arrow, returning to his hand, brought up the ring. Taking the jewel, he handed it to the princes, whose astonishment and delight knew no bounds. "What can we do for you? What can we do?" they cried. The Brahman's face had grown grave again. "Tell Bhishma, your guardian, that Drona is here," he answered briefly, and relapsed again into the depths of thought.

The lads trooped off, with their enthusiasm fresh upon them, to describe to Bhishma, the Protector, the extraordinary experience of the morning; and he, struck by the thought that Drona was the very teacher he was seeking, hastened in person to see him and bring him to the palace. Bhishma had known of Drona formerly as the son of the great sage Bharadwaja. . . . Drona, after his father's death, had performed great austerities and gone through a very determined course of study, in consequence of which he had been mysteriously gifted with divine weapons and the knowledge of how to use them.

22. FROM THE HYMNS OF HOMER (CIRCA 700 BCE)

From Hugh G. Evelyn-White, ed., *Hesiod, the Homeric Hymns, and Homerica* (London: Heinemann, 1914), 456.

The Homeric Hymns are ancient texts praising the gods of the ancient Greeks. They are about 2,700 years old. This particular selection shows a common practice in history, naming the Earth Mother.

Hymn to the Earth Mother—A Homeric Poem

I will sing of well-founded Earth, mother of all, eldest of all beings.
She feeds all creatures that are in the world,
all that go upon the goodly land,
and all that are in the paths of the seas, and all that fly:
all these are fed of her store.
Through you, O queen, men are blessed in their children
and blessed in their harvests,
and to you it belongs to give means of life to mortal men
and to take it away.
Happy is the man whom you delight to honour!
He has all things abundantly:
his fruitful land is laden with corn,
his pastures are covered with cattle,
and his house is filled with good things.
Such men rule orderly in their cities of fair women:
great riches and wealth follow them:
their sons exult with everfresh delight,
and their daughters with flower-laden hands
play and skip merrily over the soft flowers of the field.
Thus it is with those whom you honour
O holy goddess, bountiful spirit.
Hail, Mother of the gods, wife of starry Heaven;
freely bestow upon me for this my song substance that cheers the heart!
And now I will remember you and another song also.

Glossary

abstract thinking The ability many scientists maintain defines the behavior of modern humans.

accident In the comparative method, one of the three possible explanations for coincidence. *See also* borrowing; shared descent.

Aghajari, Hashem Iranian reformer and historian imprisoned for his humanist ideas.

anatomically modern human The physically modern person.

animism The belief that all things have spirit or life.

archetype A motif or symbol that appears universally.

argument An opinion supported by evidence.

assertion An opinion not supported by evidence.

Atlantic World A genre of historical study.

Battle of Marathon Battle between Athenians and Persians around 2,500 years ago.

behaviorally modern human The intellectually modern human.

big history The study of the history of the whole of the universe, including human history.

Blombos Cave Location in southern Africa of early behaviorally modern humans.

borrowing In the comparative method, one of the three possible explanations for coincidence. *See also* accident; shared descent.

Brahman A member of a Hindu class; more specifically, a priest from that class.

Buddhism Religion following the mystical teaching of Buddha.

Campbell, Joseph Scholar of myths.

capital and labor Marxist categories of social and economic history.

capitalism Economic system employing free market, private property, and profit motive.

causality Patterns of cause and effect.

Celtic An Indo-European language group and people of western Europe, including Irish.

citizen A person owing allegiance to and entitled to protection from a government.

Code of Hammurabi Ancient codified law.

codified Written, usually in reference to a law.

collective responsibility When citizens are responsible and accountable for the actions of a state (government).

comparative method A scientific method of comparison.

Confucius Chinese philosopher.

Creasy, Sir Edward Nineteenth-century British historian.

creation myth A universal type of myth describing the origins of a people, humanity, or the universe.

critical thinking To examine in context and comparison, using reason.

Declaration of the Rights of Man and of the Citizen Statement of independence and the establishment of the democratic nation, from the French Revolution, 1789.

determinism A theory of predictable patterns.

Dickens, Charles English author; novels described conditions during English industrialization.

diviner In ancient traditions, a doctor who heals by communicating with spirits.

economic determinism The argument of economics and structures as historical determinants.

egalitarian Promoting human equality.

Eiffel Tower Tower in Paris, symbol of the modern age and the power of industry.

Engels, Friedrich Advocate of workers' rights in nineteenth-century England and Germany.

Enlightenment Era of the advance of social humanist philosophy, particularly in France.

First Language The original human language.

freedom The first element of humanism and of human rights.

French Revolution Revolt of French citizens against the Old Regime in 1789. Proposed "liberty, equality, and fraternity" to replace the feudal class system.

Galileo Galilei Seventeenth-century Italian astronomer, indicted by the Inquisition in 1633.

Gandhi, Mahatma Reformer of India who opposed English colonization using passive resistance.

genre An area of historical study.

Germanic A family of Indo-European languages and associated cultures, including English, German, and others.

globalization The growing connectedness, economically and otherwise, of the world as technology reduces time and space.

Great Men and Battles A method of historical analysis, largely out of date.

hero myth A myth that follows a particular pattern of separation, initiation, and return.

heroic man Classical Greek ideal of the humanist man who pursues and defines his own fate even in defiance of the gods.

Hildegard of Bingen German nun of the twelfth century.

historical Supportable by evidence.

Holocaust deniers Those asserting that evidence for Holocaust against the Jews is insufficient.

Human Rights Watch Organization investigating labor abuses, particularly against children.

humanism The principle that individuals are born free and equal and the preference for acting (publicly) on reason above belief.

Hymn to the Nile Ancient Egyptian prayer.

inclusive To include rather than exclude; can be used to measure the degree to which a society is democratic.

Indo-European The world's largest family of languages.

industrialization The use of human, animal, and natural power with machine power.

Islam The religion and body of followers of Muhammad.

King, Martin Luther, Jr. American organizer and advocate for passive resistance against human rights abuses in the United States.

The Kingdom of God Is within You Leo Tolstoy's book on a Christian's obligation for noncompliance with violence.

Kipling, Rudyard English author of the British colonial experience in India.

Latin A family of Indo-European languages and associated cultures including French, Italian, Spanish, and others.

League of Nations Organization established after the First World War to provide a world forum for diplomacy and dialogue.

Luther, Martin Saxon reformer of the sixteenth century. Luther translated the Bible into German.

Mahabharata Sacred text and myth of India.

Marx, Karl German economic philosopher of the nineteenth century.

material culture Food, clothing, and shelter.

Maya People of Mesoamerica, ancient and modern.

mead An ancient alcoholic drink made from honey.

Middle English The ancestral language to Modern English, descended from Old English.

Mother Earth A traditional association of the earth with the feminine divine.

Mount Fuji Japanese mountain and site of Buddhist pilgrimage.

Muhammad In Islam, the messenger or prophet of God.

mysticism Belief in the unity of all things in God; a universal religious principle.

myth Story that carries a truth or grand meaning but may or may not be historically authentic.

nationalism Support for one's own nation.

nation-state A people (nation) organized around an independent state.

Normans "Norsemen" who brought French Norman to the British Isles in 1066.

the Other An outsider.

papal Relating to the office of the pope, bishop of Rome.

Paradox of Genealogy The illusion that ancestry is unique, not shared.

Pico (Giovanni Pico della Mirandola) Fifteenth-century Italian humanist.

philosophes Advocates and writers, usually French, of the Enlightenment.

Popul Vuh Sacred text and myth of the Kiche Maya.

primary sources Sources produced or used by the people under investigation.

propaganda Information used to advocate or further a cause; also information used to damage an opposing cause.

Protestant Reformation Early modern challenges to the Roman church and some of its teachings, resulting in the establishment of new church denominations.

Qur'an Sacred text of Islam.

Renaissance Fifteenth-century "revival" of Greek humanism, particularly in art.

revisionism Revision of historical interpretation on the basis of new argument.

The Salvation Army Nineteenth-century charity organization established in response to abuses of industrialism and capitalism in England.

Sanskrit Indo-European language of India and the sacred language of Hindus.

Saxons and Angles Germanic tribes whose languages are ancestors to English.

scientific method Systematic method of inquiry requiring objective measurements and testing.

Scientific Revolution The revolutions in scientific thought led by Newton, Galileo, and others, leading to a widespread acceptance in Europe and North America of modern scientific methods and laws.

secondary sources Commentary on primary sources; historical arguments.

self-determination The right of a people (nation) to determine its own government, policies, and so on.

shared descent In the comparative method, one of the three possible explanations for coincidence. *See also* accident; borrowing.

shared fate Twentieth-century reality that one country's war, economy, and human rights record affects other countries or all countries around the world.

Shona A people of Africa, ancient and modern.

Silk Road Networks of land and sea trade routes spanning much of Asia and eastern Europe; used for centuries to connect societies from Japan to Italy and all points in between. Also refers to the migratory and cosmopolitan culture along the Silk Road.

Slavic A family of Indo-European languages and associated cultures including Czech, Polish, Russian, and others.

The Starry Messenger Galileo's book on the position of the planets in relation to the sun.

Sufism Mystical tradition within Islam.

Sunnah Second sacred text of Islam.

Teotihuacan Ancient people of Mesoamerica, with an advanced technology but no writing.

unhistorical Not supported by evidence.

United Nations Voluntary organization of world states established after the Second World War to provide a forum for world mediation.

universals Aspects of culture found in all societies.

Vandals Germanic tribe of the ancient period.

Western tradition A controversial term referring to a set of literary, scientific, political, artistic, and philosophical principles, influenced by Greco-Roman and Christian traditions, that set "the West" apart from other civilizations. Most countries associated with the Western tradition either are European or have been strongly influenced by West European immigration or settlement, such as the Americas and Australasia.

Xuanzang Chinese pilgrim to India.

Zimbabwe Central African culture.

Zionists Proponents of a Jewish national state.

Zulu A Bantu people and culture of southeastern Africa.

About the Author

David Hertzel is professor of history at Southwestern Oklahoma State University.